CISO LEADERSHIP
CYBER SECURITY TOP COP
First Edition

Authored by Del Alfred, MBA

Contributions from Sameer Sait, PLD

Library of Congress Control Number: 2014918628
CreateSpace Independent Publishing Platform, North
Charleston, SC

ISBN-10: 0692297391

TABLE OF CONTENTS

Table of Contents

Preface

As organizations, people and "things" get connected in ways that we never imagined possible, they become increasingly susceptible to cyber attacks, misrepresentations and willful compromise. This book focuses on the important leadership tenets and capabilities that are critical for leaders responsible for overall information security and risk management. The existing mind-set of juxtaposing information security leaders with physical security or information technology is moot. Information security is no longer a niche role and all organizations must start engaging in the practice of sound information management principles, one of which is protecting the digital assets of the organization.

With the growing demand for data to drive everything from strategic decision making to operational activities, there is an incremental value in obtaining this data for a variety of players. The data constructs can lead to immediate benefit (credit card fraud, unauthorized access to products or services etc.) or a sustained competitive advantage (reputation damage, loss of market confidence, intellectual property loss etc.

Organizations often fail to realize that risk increases exponentially (and in direct proportion) to both the volume and sensitivity of data being collected. As a security leader thinks through his or her strategy on information security, the mindset needs to shift from technical controls management to building a "risk-aware" organization that is in tune with the evolving threat landscape. By establishing the appropriate information risk mindset across the enterprise, the information security leader can position the enterprise for success in an increasingly connected business landscape.

This book will enable security leaders to define, develop and maintain core security competencies that adapt to changing business needs. More importantly, as the threat landscape evolves, security leaders should have the foresight to structure their organizations for continued success.

This page was intentionally left blank

About the Authors

Del Alfred, CISSP, CSSLP has been both a practitioner and leader in Information Security for over 15 years. He is recognized as a business visionary with hands-on experience managing and securing the information assets for multi-billion dollar enterprises. His track record of success in creating robust and secure technology platforms that allow for innovation has proven to be instrumental in driving success across the enterprise.

Alfred's deep technical expertise combined with his business acumen has allowed him to develop and mentor information security leaders at some of the largest and most successful firms across the nation.

Sameer Sait, CISSP, PMP has spent the majority of his career building governance, risk & compliance programs at fortune 500 firms. Wearing the hats of both a security strategist and risk manager, his approach transcends traditional cyber detection/ protection capabilities by focusing on building "risk aware" organizations. He has a degree in Information Systems Management from Carnegie Mellon University and has completed the Program for Leadership Development (PLD) at Harvard Business School.

Chapter 1

CISO Transformation Leadership Framework

The Chief Information Security Officer (CISO) is the senior most information security and risk professional in an organization. Becoming a CISO takes a unique type of transformational leadership and a strong understanding of information risk as a broad domain. The aspects of risk and security are deeply rooted in human behavior; with large components being non-technical focused. An effective CISO takes into account intangibles that allow for influence without always having command and control type situations. In order to accomplish this unique and often times, hybrid approach to leadership, the CISO needs to effectively change the way an organization thinks, executes, produces and scales.

The transformational leadership tenets for information security are: having <u>strong business acumen,</u> being an <u>effective coalition builder</u>, using <u>macro and micro communication</u>, being a <u>change agent</u>, being <u>results-driven,</u> strongly advocating for <u>beginning to end quality of service,</u> and <u>leading people</u>. The synergy of these traits building on each other make up transformational leadership, based on the Information Security Transformational Leadership Framework. These different traits can be grouped into Education, Establishment, Execution, and Effectiveness.

Contrary to popular belief, these leadership tenets should come first before the technological aspects that are traditionally considered to be key to information security.

As a transformational leader, the CISO represents scalable thought leadership for progressive organizations that must balance much of their trust against the rising tide of security uncertainty.

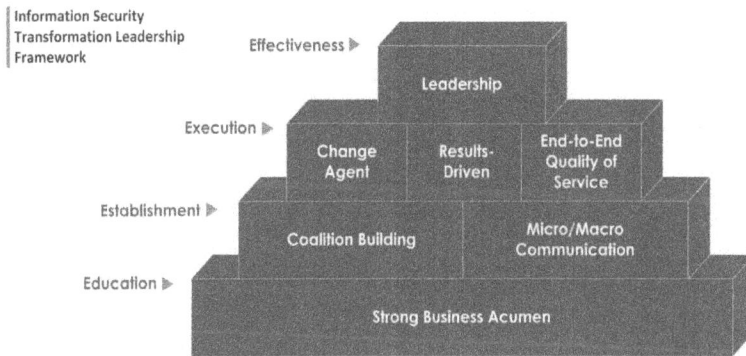

Strong Business Acumen

One of the biggest issues CISOs are currently grappling with is that they need to become progressive business enablers. In the past, CISO's have used their peer group of security professionals to be their benchmark for determining which skills are essential to succeed. Now, that benchmark has become the security team essentials while the CISOs have transitioned into business executive roles. CISOs need to compare themselves to their new peer group – the other executives sitting in the boardroom. Based on this comparison, it has become essential that strong business acumen is necessary for success.

Business acumen is the ability to understand and deal with a business situations based on the knowledge of the financial, marketing, and operational functions of an organization. Some related characteristics include executive-level thinking, business sense, financial literacy, and business management. These involve understanding the key drivers of the business and how they are tied to profitable growth, understanding how the business makes and loses money, being aware of the different dimensions of business issues, and being able to think strategically.

Instead of thinking about what an application does and how great its features are, CISOs must assess the impact of the technology on the business. As the business begins to evaluate new technologies to support business processes and organizational growth, they will be looking at the rewards of these technologies and how these will benefit the organization from a functional perspective with very little to no regard for information risks. On the flipside, CISOs will have to help the business understand the security risks that these new technologies introduce into the organization so that the organization can navigate risk and make sound decisions on technology selection and implementation.

One of the most illustrative examples of this would be the security around tablets and mobile devices. Many organizations are thinking about ways this technology can improve collaboration, aid sales, maximize performance, and increase productivity. However, the CISO will need to be able to communicate how these technologies expose the business to risk, and how they need to be implemented to maintain compliance with regulatory requirements and industry standards.

Understanding the key components of the organization – not just its security – is what will set a great CISO apart from the rest if he or she is better able to relate to the business units. To be a key player in business innovation, CISOs must know the core business processes and the associated risks inside out. This includes understanding the business environment, the technology that enables the business, the issues and risks, the competition and the market, and the customers.

Knowing the Business

Knowing the business involves gaining a detailed understanding of the business objectives, strategies, and performance plans. This includes sales targets, areas of growth, sources of profit, and so on. Examples of specific things a CISO can do are to read the company's business strategy plans, attend strategy meetings, and speak to the business managers about their goals. In each of these, evaluate the risk implications and determine how to best manage the risks.

Knowing the Technology that Enables the Business

In today's world, technology is embedded in the operational processes of any business. It permeates throughout the organization, enabling processes for developing and managing products/services. Understanding the role of technology in critical operations provides insight into areas of relevant technology risk, which again ties back to the business. Vulnerabilities and potential threats related to technology are ultimately vulnerabilities of and potential threats to the business.

Knowing the Competition and the Market

External factors such as competition and the market influence the organization's ability to drive revenue and profitability. Understanding the environment in which the business operates is, thus, critical to seeing the big picture and making decisions accordingly, as well as understanding decisions made by the business. By being aware of the external environment, CISOs are also better able to anticipate the future, whether it is in the form of an opportunity or a threat, which allows for improved strategic planning.

Knowing the Customers

Customers are the backbone of any company– the more

customers an organization has, the more money made.

Understanding who the customers are and what they want

is another critical element of business acumen. In order to

create products and services that sell, organizations must

first know who to sell to. This knowledge should directly

influence activities such as customer risk management,

strategic planning and decision-making, as well as product

development and management.

In addition to these facets of business acumen, CISOs

must also keep in mind that consultative business skills are

paramount to having business acumen. Consultative

business skills allow a CISO to speak the language of

business without excessive technical jargon by working

with people and exchanging ideas through multiple

channels of communication and actively listening to the varied perspective presented.

While many business leaders have advanced in their approach towards information security, many still place their focus on risk as that is one of the primary responsibilities of executive leadership – to provide stewardship through business risk management. Therefore, a common language format for the CISO would be to present ideas in the context of information risk management. Presenting ideas in this format where risk is front and center gives executives a sense of comfort in an area in which they are familiar and gives the CISO a platform where the executives can remain focused on what both enables and impedes the business. Business leaders are not usually wired to discuss information security, but instead discuss business risks. It is what they understand since they make risk decisions every day.

When things are viewed from a business perspective and security framed within a business context, it is easier for business leaders to get the point being made. Examples of this are conveying benefits that mean something to them, such as faster times to market, reductions in costs, and improved operational efficiencies. All of these skills help a great CISO become a trusted business partner.

Coalition Building

It is one thing to have security strategies in mind, but converting plans into action requires organizational influence. That's why it's critical to develop strong working relationships with fellow business leaders in every facet of the business such as operations, finance, legal, and marketing. Silos and compartmentalized functions make it difficult to manage risk proactively. It is essential to have risk decisions made collaboratively among technical security experts, general risk and control experts, and business-aligned non-specialists. All fulfill front-line business roles but, in dialogue with the CISO and security professionals, add that indispensable and invaluable perspective on where the real business value is that needs protection, as well as what degree of security control imposes an acceptable burden on the business.

An important part of maintaining this dialogue is shedding information security's reputation as an innovation roadblock. If information security is collaborating side by side with other business functions, initiatives can be shaped from the outset. To really integrate information security into the company's business innovation process, to be there for new initiatives and add significant value, one has to be

able to influence his or her business colleagues.

Coalition Building with
Management, Business, and
Staff

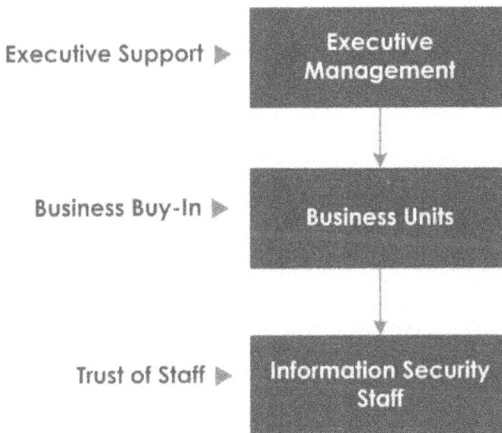

Executive Support ▶ **Executive Management**

Business Buy-In ▶ **Business Units**

Trust of Staff ▶ **Information Security Staff**

Beyond general support for the security mandate,

executive management can help champion security's role in

specific projects. Executive support is critical – once it is

secured, business buy-in and staff trust will follow more

easily. Good allies can be found throughout the executive

ranks, even in relatively unexpected places. Look for

projects wherein value can be delivered for a specific executive –the head of human resources, for example. Often, security can add considerable value to enterprise-wide projects involving the management of employees and contractors. Security can help manage a global workforce by increasing efficiencies in onboarding and off boarding, and complying with international privacy regulations.

But, as mentioned, executive leadership is only one facet. CISOs need to build relationships at all levels of the organization and be able to convince the key people who are driving the business of specific contributions that can be made. Once convinced, CISOs can gain the kind of access and involvement needed, and ultimately be in a position to apply programs, systems, and services that drive value. Understanding the organization well enough to know where one can leverage influence – that is, knowing who to convince in order to sway others – is critical.

A great tool to use to focus efforts is charting people's power and influence versus their support for security. This involves identifying the key people within the organization – some individuals will be senior managers, while others could be influential individuals. Actually go through an exercise and plot them on the chart, with the vertical axis representing organizational influence and the horizontal reflecting support for security. Individuals that end up in the top right hand quadrant are already strong supporters of security, and very high influencers in the organization. These are important relationships to safeguard and nurture. For influencers who are not currently strong supporters, define a strategy to convert them to the top-right quadrant. Other key players may be supporters who currently do not have much power and influence yet, but may eventually.

Develop those relationships so that as their influence within

the organization rises, their support for security also grows.[1]

Relationship building requires face-to-face interaction.

This is the case for all stakeholders. Frequently meeting

with individuals in the business is important for

maintaining these relationships.

Micro and Macro Communication

The ability to communicate effectively has always been

a core competency for any business executive, and today's

CISO is fast becoming just that. The CISO's role is

evolving and moving out of Information Technology (IT);

its responsibilities and focus are shifting from IT risk to

business risk. As with other executives, the company

---

[1] EMC. *The Time is Now: Making Information Security Strategic to Business Innovation.* Retrieved from http://www.emc.com/collateral/industry-overview/rsa-strategic-security-wo-mountain-print.pdf.

expects the CISO to create value. A common language is needed for the business and the security organization. It needs to reflect a communication style that serves the business, the CISO, and external parties.

Effective communication from the CISO means having a wide range of knowledge, understanding the interests of the business, and the ability to apply this knowledge. CISOs need to be aware of how security is perceived, understood, and supported at every level of the organization, as well as outside of it. This part of the CISO mission requires clear communication, clear reporting, and an ability to deliver crisp messages that can help audiences internalize and quickly accept the information.

Micro Communication (Internal)
To build a stable position, earn credibility and create an impact, it is essential to have a solid understanding of how

to communicate the value of security activities to a wide range of security consumers, as well as communication tools and reporting capabilities versatile enough to support communication objectives. In order for a security program to be implemented such that it functions effectively, one must be able to get that message across to everyone. For example, one should not expect to communicate with the technical operations team the way he or she would with a business leader. When communicating with business leaders and executives, program reporting is key. Program reporting or reporting the results and status of a program is one important method of communication. One must be able to select and adapt communication style according to the target audience. Figuring out the different business lingo and determining how to translate what is expected into a language that the business understands is crucial.

What, where, and how one communicates about security within his or her organization needs to take different forms depending on which security constituent he or she is trying to reach. Some factors to consider include whether one is addressing senior corporate executives at the C-suite level, business unit leadership, or IT staff; the specific method of delivery being used such as email, a comprehensive report, or a weekly planning meeting; whether one is communicating in action and behavior, as well as through written and electronic means; whether one is training, coaching and mentoring security staff to extend, support, and explain the communications objectives that have been defined, etc.

Understanding how each security constituent looks at his or her job objectives is necessary. From this perspective, imagine how each views security's effectiveness in supporting his or her role in driving the organization's agenda. For example, if a CISO seeks to raise the CEO's security awareness, remember that the CEO is primarily focused on the drivers behind earnings, profitability, and shareholder value. This person may be more receptive if one can explicitly link security with a role in supporting these key objectives. As a CISO, addressing the CFO, it is important to be prepared to discuss security in the language and context of financial issues, such as security's current and future impact on the corporation's assets, liabilities, income, and expenses. Points one might consider bringing to the table are how the security strategy addresses risk management, and its short- and long-term effects on the company's share price. When working with the COO, expect to discuss how security should support new product or service strategies, or how security will impact operational availability, business process integrity, or continuous operational improvement.

Security executives can streamline communication between senior management and security personnel by using a common language. Eliminating technical jargon from the conversation ensures that concerns and objectives are correctly understood by all parties, thus, synchronizing the company's strategic initiatives with its security systems. Executives outside the field of security are concerned with how proposed changes will affect their operations. Security officers should therefore have enough business knowledge to put security in terms others can understand and appreciate.

Take the time to develop good skills in listening, conversing and exchanging information with other business and IT leaders. Take an interest in their points of view and build rapport at a personal level.

Macro Communication (External)

Communicating with external parties such as law enforcement and the media requires a certain level of composure and discretion. CISOs will typically be in this position as part of crisis management more than public relations or marketing, but regardless of the purpose of communication, a CISO will want to cultivate a strong, positive image of the organization to external parties. Care must be exercised in what information is provided to external parties, particularly since the CISO is not representing merely himself, but the organization as well.

When communicating, avoid being defensive or aggressive. This kind of behavior reflects negatively on both the CISO and the company. By avoiding being on the defense or on the attack, one will be able to stay objective, clear-headed, and open-minded. This makes it easier to think about what the other person is saying, and allow one to formulate an effective response.

In responding to external parties, respond accurately and avoid ambiguity, but do not provide information that should remain confidential. Various groups will rely on the CISO for the story, but this doesn't mean divulging confidential information. Answer questions directly and do not beat around the bush; if one cannot disclose something, simply state that it is confidential. Ensure that the groups engaged leave with sufficient information to produce an accurate report.

Additionally, set expectations with the public. For instance, if being asked for information on an information security incident, communicate how the company is responding and what specific actions items they have committed to, including the timeline. By conveying this commitment to customers and other external groups, CISOs, in effect, are providing them the assurance they need, and acting accountably. This is critical to maintaining the integrity of the company.

Change Agent

Every day, information flows into and out of companies, enabling real-time analysis in support of decision-making. Businesses today rely on this influx and exchange of information to compete and operate more intelligently. Employees, vendors, and business associates located in different parts of the world are all connected across a web of technologies, working in collaboration to deliver products and services to customers. However, these extensive, interweaving networks, despite all their benefits, also create a host of vulnerabilities that present information security challenges. As the supporting infrastructure grows more complex, and as information comes in from and goes out through more and more channels, the function of protecting a company's information assets gets more and more challenging. For example, a study by Kaspersky Labs reports that 91 percent of enterprise smart phone users connect to corporate email, but only one in three is required to install mobile security software.[2] CISOs struggle with these issues and questions, all within their organizational context. Is it even possible in this day and age where everybody is connected, and everything is wide open, to effectively secure company's information assets? The answer is yes – but it does not come easily. Effective

---

[2] Kaspersky Labs. *Enterprise Mobile Survey*. Retrieved from http://usa.kaspersky.com/sites/usa.kaspersky.com/files/Enterprise%20 Mobile%20Survey.pdf

information security requires fundamental changes not only in processes, but in individual attitudes and organizational behavior as well.

As many CISOs are already aware, change is not the easiest sell. It can be very challenging for organizations to change. In fact, it may take years and even decades for organizations to mature, primarily because employees are generally set in their ways and can be very resistant to change. While this may hold true for lots of companies, it is not impossible to achieve an organizational paradigm shift in terms of how the company and its employees perceive Information Security.

Organizational perception of Information Security is one of the most fundamental things that must change. Information Security is often seen as a roadblock in organizations, where employees and managers do not have an appreciation of the role and benefits of information

security. This change must start with expanding the mission

of information security, from technical and business

employees and their machines to include everyone who

does business with the company. Since each person poses a

potential breach, each one must also represent a piece of

the solution. In the end, success depends on creating a risk-

aware culture. "A risk-aware culture represents a new way

of thinking, one in which a pragmatic approach to security

informs every decision and procedure at every level of the

company. This must recast the way people handle

information, from the C-suite to summer interns. In such a

culture, secure procedures for data become second nature,

much like fastening a seat belt or storing matches in a safe

place."[3]

---

[3] IBM. *Security Essentials for CIOs*. Retrieved from
http://instituteforadvancedsecurity.com/content-

CISOs are generally in a good position to facilitate change and establish the type of environment that establishes what information security really means, as well as developing a risk-aware culture. In order to usher in this change, CISOs must also be able to provide the confidence and assurance needed for an organization to be open to change. However, this becomes difficult as CISOs, at the onset, often find themselves fighting fires with insufficient resources and without a full understanding of their organizations. Without a broad understanding of the organization, CISOs will be unable to effectively institute change or implement solutions since these solutions attempt to deal with symptoms instead of the root cause, and offer no real and lasting value to the organization as a whole.

---

library/m/public_files/185/download.aspx.

To be an effective change agent, CISOs must allot time to fully immerse themselves in the organization and its processes, in order to understand the various business functions, what the business values, and what it takes for them to succeed and produce the output needed for the overall success of the organization. Understanding the big picture is the foundation on which CISOs are able to drive change.

Effective CISOs champion change by driving consensus and motivating people through a series of sound principles within the context of the organization. Some of these principles include valuing perspectives, building multicultural teams, and providing a platform for diversity and inclusion. Paramount to leading people is the CISO's ability to follow the organization through changes, follow leadership goals that enable the business to function as a single unit, and offer the right temperament needed for sustainability of operations.

A CISO seeking to be a change agent for an organization must not only overcome perceptions that are erroneous but also manage expectations where they properly apply. It also requires the ability to effectively communicate with the CEO in that just as he assumes risk for the business at large, the CISO assumes all risks associated with the information assets the business values and needs to protect. CISOs need to communicate with C-level executives in words they understand; in particular, how the information security function helps them to reduce risk and protect the company's interests. By framing information security as an approach to reducing risk, CISOs are in a much better position to relate with business leaders. Communication is covered in greater detail later in *Macro and Micro Communication.*

Results-Driven

Let us say the CISO has just been asked to formalize the information security function for his or her company. The task involves creating the structures and processes to govern information security. Until now, security had been an unspoken expectation – an inefficient and risky approach that produced inconsistent results.

Or maybe the CISO is trying to gain executive buy-in for a security initiative, and executive management asks for formally defined measures of success.

Or perhaps the Board of Directors has been increasing funding for information security and making it more of a priority.

All of these scenarios will involve measuring results. This will help to answer questions such as: has the decision helped the organization to achieve a competitive advantage?; are we spending enough on security or are we spending too much?; what are the goals of the initiative and how will we know if it is successful?; has security improved in the past year, etc. Security metrics can answer all these questions and many more

A widely accepted management principle is that an activity cannot be managed if it cannot be measured. Security is no different. In the US National Institute of Standards and Technology (NIST) publication *Security Metrics Guide for Information Technology Systems*,[4] the word "metrics" is defined as follows:

[4] Swanson, M.; N. Bartol; J. Sabato; J. Hash; L. Graffo. (2005). *Security Metrics Guide for Information Technology Systems* (NIST Special Publication 800-55). USA: National Institute of Standards and Technology. Retrieved from

> Metrics are tools designed to facilitate decision-making and improve performance and accountability through collection, analysis and reporting of relevant performance-related data. The purpose of measuring performance is to monitor the status of measured activities and facilitate improvement in those activities by applying corrective actions, based on observed measurements.

By understanding the results being sought at the beginning of any initiative, it is easier to see how much progress is being made, and how imminent the endgame is. These results are what should drive any information security initiative. When time is taken to quantify the results of an security processes through metrics and frame that information in a way that is easy to digest, CISOs will find that efforts are better understood and appreciated by business units.

---

http://csrc.nist.gov/publications/nistpubs/800-55-Rev1/SP800-55-rev1.pdf.

Metrics can be an effective tool for CISOs and security managers to analyze the effectiveness of various components of security programs such as training, the security of a specific system, and the ability of business units to address security issues. Metrics can also help assess the level of risk in not implementing a given corrective action and, thus, provide guidance in prioritizing corrective actions. With knowledge gained through metrics, CISOs are more informed and are better equipped to provide answers to difficult questions from their executives and others.

Security metrics will help drive performance improvement. Metrics exert a motivating influence on the performance of any organization in executing its information security operations. When visibility is increased and results measured in black and white, people tend to be more diligent, resulting in performance improvement.

Security metrics measure the effectiveness controls. Are controls producing the expected results? For example, are there fewer cases of non-compliant anti-virus software or non-approved software installed on machines since the monthly audit? Are more machines going through patch management now due to the controls recently implemented? Security metrics can provide proof of whether the best-laid plans are succeeding or not. With objective data to support conclusions it becomes easier to identify the weak points in any security posture, and what priorities are needed to be going forward.

Security metrics provide effective decision-making support. As demonstrated in the previous scenarios, security metrics provide guidance in decision-making.

Metrics help to identify priority areas that may require remediation, define the expected results of a specific security project, and provide assistance with budget justification.

Security metrics provide increased accountability. Since metrics are an agreed-upon baseline for making comparisons, comparing them across different areas of the organization, a high level of commitment and motivation can be achieved, creating improved results.

Security metrics can demonstrate the state of compliance. Assessing compliance with information security policies and standards and regulatory requirements becomes considerably simpler with a security metrics program in place. When stakeholders periodically review a consistent set of metrics, that visibility will drive one toward achieving information security compliance objectives.

Differentiating between metrics that are meaningful primarily to those with direct responsibility for security management and those that interact directly with the interests of executive management is critical to development of an effective security metrics program. Truly useful metrics indicate the degree to which security goals, such as confidentiality of information, are being realized, and they influence actions taken to improve an organization's overall security program.

End-to-End Quality of Service

The age of business as usual is long gone and the need for end-to-end quality of service is paramount to ensuring reasonable assurance to business processes. This involves understanding the business and the different points at which information is accessed or transmitted, seeing business initiatives through from start to finish, and being able to think strategically and look ahead to consider the ever-changing internal and external environments in which the company operates.

CISOs also must have a full understanding of the structure of the organization, from the Board of Directors and senior management down to the business lines, to service providers and vendors. Along with this organizational structure, CISOs must also understand how the company operates and its various business processes from beginning to end, as well as the different points at which information is stored, processed, and transmitted. Who has access to view or edit this information? Do they need to have access? Where does the information go? This view into the lifecycle of information, including the people, processes, and technology involved, is vital. By asking these questions, the CISO will be in a better position to identify potential vulnerabilities and secure information assets accordingly at all points throughout the business process.

By having a good grasp of the current business processes within the organization, the CISO has a better understanding of which functions are critical to the business, and which ones are relatively lower in priority, particularly from an availability standpoint, where availability refers readiness of services for immediate use. Linking business processes to supporting systems facilitates the identification of potential single points of failure, and evaluating any corrective actions, i.e. putting redundancies in place. This ensures that any disruptions to operations are mitigated, greatly improving the resiliency of the business.

Not all risks can be mitigated, however. There are some, which the company will have to choose to accept and manage. For example, it may simply be cost-prohibitive to institute certain controls. The risk being avoided may not be worth the cost. What is important is that these risk decisions are made in a reasonable manner, defensible, well thought-out, and well documented.

For new business initiatives, it is important to be involved early during the planning phases. Security must be built into existing systems and processes for proposing, reviewing, and approving business initiatives. Focus on creating fast and flexible processes that help to accelerate – not hold up – projects. Processes must be consistent across projects so that people can learn how they work. The objective is to have security built into initiatives, not tacked on at the end, early involvement in the process to ensure there is security visibility in the initiative through to the implementation and closure stage is critical to quality.

Furthermore, one must think strategically and consider developing security approaches that align with business initiatives. Strive to make traditional security operations as efficient as possible, which will allow time high-level thinking and critical security planning of initiatives.

All in all, end-to-end quality of service enables a business to deliver quality results consistently, increases efficiencies, and promotes stronger organizational consciousness.

Delivers results consistently

By reducing single points of failure, business interruptions are likewise reduced. If a part of the process or system fails, the corresponding backup component or contingency option is immediately available to take over as the primary. This allows the business and its products and services to be available to customers around the clock delivering results consistently.

Increases efficiencies

CISOs that are familiar with the processes from end to end know where the issues are (such as areas of duplicate effort or bottleneck points), and, thus, where efficiencies can be achieved or where control points should be.

Provides visibility into the attack surface

Understanding the ins and outs of operational processes and supporting technology enables the CISO to understand the attack surface. The attack surface is the areas of a service or technology where information can be compromised or a service could be disrupted or denied, i.e. any points where information can be siphoned or leaked or authorized access denied due to compromise. In other words, it refers to the points at which the company may be exposed to risk due to information entry and exit points that translate to vulnerabilities in the processes and underlying systems. Understanding where information goes and where it comes from is central to understanding the risk exposure.

Promotes stronger organizational consciousness

End-to-end service comes with an understanding, not only of the intricacies of the business and the flow of information, but of the big picture as well. Employees that recognize their responsibilities in relation to business processes from beginning to end are better equipped for improved organizational performance. Additionally, a collaborative environment is fostered when various groups throughout the company are aware of other departments that a specific process interfaces with. This knowledge also promotes improved business analysis and problem solving.

Leadership

As security and risk management become critical functions in an organization, the CISO must adopt the role of an effective leader. He or she must have the communication and leadership skills to effectively articulate the need for security to board members, the executive committee, and employees. Additionally, they must be able to represent the security team in a way that provides confidence and eases skepticism by others.

Related to this organizational skepticism, a study by the
International Data Corporation (IDC) suggests that security
concerns inhibit innovation. Respondents believed that IT
security is "the single biggest inhibitor to business
innovation," with more than 80 percent of the executives
surveyed saying they "occasionally" or "often" didn't
pursue innovative business opportunities because of
information security concerns.[5] Even more recently,
security concerns are still perceived as hindering the
adoption of certain innovative technologies, including
social technologies, electronic medical records, open
government platforms, and smart grid technologies.[6] By
shooting down ideas and standing in the way, information

---

[5] Christiansen, C. *Innovation and Security: Collaborative or
Combative*. Retrieved from
http://www.rsa.com/innovation/docs/IDC_innovation.pdf.

[6] "HP and AMD Research Shows Concerns about Security,
Technology Budgets Are Main Barrier to 'Gov 2.0'". Retrieved from
http://www.hp.com/hpinfo/newsroom/press/2012/120424c.htm

security has grown in many organizations into what IBM calls the "Department of No."[7]

Given these challenges, how can CISOs be effective leaders that are able to expand the role of information security into business operations (that is, expand the role of information security into business according to a security-by-design model, at the beginning of the project cycle, each new idea is formulated with information security risks in clear focus and the appropriate controls built into the project design)? What does it take to be a leader instead of a manager, and what is the distinction? In his 1989 book "On Becoming a Leader," Warren Bennis composed a list of the differences:

- The manager administers; the leader innovates.

[7] IBM. *Security Essentials for CIOs.* Retrieved from http://public.dhe.ibm.com/common/ssi/ecm/en/wgw03005usen/WGW0 3005USEN.PDF

- The manager is a copy; the leader is an original.

- The manager maintains; the leader develops.

- The manager focuses on systems and structure; the leader focuses on people.

- The manager relies on control; the leader inspires trust.

- The manager has a short-range view; the leader has a long-range perspective.

- The manager asks how and when; the leader asks what and why.

- The manager has his or her eye always on the bottom line; the leader's eye is on the horizon.

- The manager imitates; the leader originates.

- The manager accepts the status quo; the leader challenges it.

- The manager is the classic good soldier; the leader is his or her own person.
- The manager does things right; the leader does the right thing.

Translating these distinctions into what it means to be an effective leader as a CISO, he or she must assume a business leadership position and dispel the idea that information security is a technology support function or the "Department of No." The key to being this type of leader is the power of influence. Influential leadership incites action in others through communication and motivation. A leader of influence is one who will work to remove obstacles preventing their people from performing effectively. All leaders can get people to achieve; it takes leaders of influence to get people to want to achieve. Influential leaders focus on building constructive attitudes and drawing out talents, creating value and lasting change.

CISOs must be effective at balancing risks against rewards, in support of the business. The CISO function must encompass education and cultural change, not simply security applications and processes. CISOs will need to realign their security functions around proactive risk management instead of crisis response or incident management. And the management of information security must transition from discrete and fragmented initiatives to an integrated, systemic approach. Security has to be designed to protect the entire enterprise, not just pieces of it. By delivering these results to the business, it is more willing to place confidence in the CISO. Additionally, the most influential security leaders have a strategic voice in their enterprise. This means they have the ear of senior management, the power to convene a security or risk committee with top executives, and effective metrics for risk measurement, and to craft appropriate responses.[8]

Aside from relationships with top executives, the CISO must have confidence in his team, and they must have confidence in him. Effective leadership is not primarily based on authority, but on respectful direction and support that develops and motivates a team driven by a trusted leader. This mutual trust is paramount to the implementation of an effective security program.

Good leaders should also be able to take some risks and set trends or adopt ideas at an early stage. Others recognize a thought leader for having progressive and innovative ideas. Effective CISOs effect change through

---

[8] IBM. *Security Essentials for CIOs.* Retrieved from http://public.dhe.ibm.com/common/ssi/ecm/en/wgw03005usen/WGW03005USEN.PDF

effective communication, influence, and clarity of purpose

and direction, even if that direction is entirely new and

involves a different perspective that may not exactly be

mainstream.

Chapter 2

Governance and Organization of Cyber Security

Executive management and boards are increasingly interested in the effectiveness of information security controls, processes, and governance structures within an organization. This is evident in the rising visibility of the CISO as well as the expansion of the responsibilities that security departments are taking on. These include application security, risk management, and business continuity functions. Given the span of information security across the organization, it is critical that the various activities and functions that fall under the umbrella arc organized to facilitate good governance. Governance is the responsibility of executives and the Board of Directors, and consists of the leadership, organizational structures, and processes that ensure that the enterprise's IT and information security functions sustain and extend the organization's strategies and objectives. Borrowing from the CObIT control framework,[9] good governance presents the following benefits:

- Making a link between IT and security and business requirements
- Organizing IT and security activities into a generally accepted process model
- Identifying the major IT and security resources to be leveraged
- Defining the control objectives to be considered

---

[9] ISACA. *COBIT 4.1.*

The CISO role has evolved from a primary technical position to one that combines both technical and managerial functions. Information security has become an organizational imperative, driven by various internal and external factors. The CIO, general counsel, internal auditors, executive management, and other groups throughout the organization are directing more attention to this function now more than ever. Building a relationship and consensus with these groups is critical to the continued effectiveness information security. Today's security professionals work closely with departments such as HR, legal, audit, IT, and other functional areas to mitigate risk. This also addresses to the desired shift in the organizational perception of information security as a business roadblock to a risk management function that serves to protect data and ultimately, the business.

How can this growing set of responsibilities be organized and coordinated as part of effective information security governance? First it must be understood how these responsibilities are tied together as part of a larger framework. Translating the CObIT[10] framework into the context of information security for effective governance it is useful to understand the controls, activities, and risks that need to be managed according to four domains: 1) plan and organize, 2) acquire and implement, 3) deliver and support, and 4) monitor and evaluate.

Plan and Organize.

This domain encompasses strategy and ensuring the alignment of IT and information security with business objectives. The business strategy must be carefully

---

[10] ISACA. *COBIT 4.1*

planned, communicated, and meticulously managed. This domain addresses the following topics:

- Strategic alignment with the business strategy

- Optimum use of organizational resources

- Understanding and management of risks

One of the key processes in this domain involves managing human resources such that competent and motivated personnel develop and deliver services according to business needs. Driven primarily by legal and regulatory compliance, hiring first-rate information security staff is critical to mitigating risks that can adversely affect an organization's reputation, violate privacy, or result in the theft or destruction of information. This domain encompasses activities such as hiring and training personnel, assigning roles that correspond with skills, defining a personnel evaluation process, and ensuring that personnel are aware of their roles, responsibilities, and the dependence of the organization on them.

A competent workforce is acquired and maintained for the creation and delivery of IT and security services to the business. This is achieved by following formalized practices supporting recruiting, training, evaluating performance, promoting and terminating. This process is crucial, as people are vital assets, and governance and the internal control environment rely heavily on the motivation and competence of personnel.

Acquire and Implement.

As part of realizing the IT and information security strategy, controls and solutions must be identified, developed, and built into the business processes. This domain addresses the following topics:

- Implementation of controls and solutions that meet business needs

- Management of projects related to IT and information security

- Change control as part of implementation to minimize business interruptions

Security controls must be integrated into the systems and other process components of business operations. This effort requires securing resources such as personnel, hardware, software, and other services, which must be performed according to defined procedures for managing projects, as well as selecting and contracting with vendors (see section on *Third Party Security Management*) up to actual implementation. This ensures that the required resources are put in place in a timely and cost-effective manner.

Once a solution has been acquired or developed and implemented, an ongoing major objective of this domain is to ensure that users are satisfied with how operations and information security controls are running. The foundation is to ensure that systems and related controls are operational and used correctly by users. This requires developing documentation and providing training in order to transfer knowledge of processes and supporting systems. Knowledge must be transferred to management, end users and operations and support staff in order to facilitate ownership and responsibility over the systems and data, effective and efficient use of systems that support business processes, and the support and maintenance of these systems.

Deliver and Support.

This domain pertains to the delivery of required

services to the business, including service delivery and

assurance, service support for users, and management of

data and operational facilities. The following topics are

included:

- Delivery of IT and information security services

  according to business priorities

- Effective use of systems and enablement of

  business processes by users

- Achievement of confidentiality, integrity, and

  availability objectives

Linked to the previous domain, the *Deliver and Support*

domain highlights education and training as a critical

component for service support and delivery, as well as the

effective use of systems and performance of duties. A good

training program increases effective use of technology by reducing errors made by users, improving productivity, and increasing compliance with controls. The learning needs of each user group must first be identified, considering factors such as competence profiles, how they interact with the process and/or system, corporate culture, delivery methods, etc. By understanding the specific needs of each group, training and education materials can be customized accordingly to be more effective.

Upon completion of training delivery, the learning experience must be evaluated by the user groups for relevance, quality, effectiveness, knowledge retention, and value. The results of this evaluation should serve as input for future curriculum definition and the delivery of training sessions (see *Information Security Awareness and Training*).

Monitor and Evaluate

Processes and controls must be periodically evaluated to ensure quality and compliance with requirements, as part of performance management, internal control monitoring, governance, and regulatory compliance. This domain addresses the following topics:

- Measurement of performance as part of problem detection (see *Information Security Reporting and Metrics)*

- Ensuring effectiveness and efficiency of internal controls

- Alignment of performance with business objectives

- Achievement of confidentiality, integrity, and availability objectives

Organization

How all these facets of the information security

function are organized and assigned depend on the type of

security organization. Generally speaking, there are some

core security functions that will be hard to implement in a

decentralized environment, but many other functions can

easily exist at the business-unit level.

Typically, the security risk and IT architecture roles are

best handled in a centralized model, while the operations

role can be decentralized to the business unit or geographic

division. A completely decentralized security and risk

organization is only ideal for organizations with extremely

autonomous business units that have very different security

needs. For most organizations, however, a centralized

security group will provide improved consistency, control,

and influence.

Centralized Model

To improve alignment across business units across the organization, information security governance can be structured based on a centralized model. There is a central governance body dedicated to information security functions. Overseen by the CISO, this group is principally responsible for activities such as creating policies, investigating incidents, conducting security risk assessments, and planning and implementing security controls. All business units are required to abide by the policies and standards set forth by the central group.

To ensure alignment across business units, using a centralized model would typically be more effective. Having a central governance body overseeing and managing the information security program would help ensure that business units adhere to policies and procedures. This structure lends better oversight to executive leadership since the organization's security posture can be evaluated from a central standpoint. Centralized governance is generally most efficient as resources can be leveraged in a cost-effective manner across the organization, minimizing duplication of effort and better utilizing resources. Finally, should an incident occur, it can be handled using a consistent approach under corporate oversight.

Centralized Model of
Information Security
Governance

BOARD

CISO

Information Security

Policy Development
Program Development and Oversight
Incident Investigation
Controls Planning and Implementation

Business Unit   **Business Unit**   **Business Unit**

Hybrid Model

The best of the centralized and decentralized models is

achieved by providing for a central governance body

focused on program results, while the business unit has

control over the methods. These groups work together to

achieve the overall program objectives. To improve

accountability while leveraging the benefits of the

independence of the business unit, the information security

group, overseen by the CISO, is established to create organizational standards for information security, with input from the business units. Shareholders expect management to be well versed on how the organization manages risks, especially those in relation to information security. For example, following an information security breach, senior managers will typically be called upon to report on the incident. In a hybrid model, these managers will be much more familiar with information security policies and procedures, since they provided input on their development.

Business units are responsible for creating their own information security procedures that comply with these standards and general policies, as well as implementing and managing security controls. Shared responsibilities between the information security group and the business unit include developing baseline requirements and monitoring the

effectiveness of controls as part of achieving program

objectives.

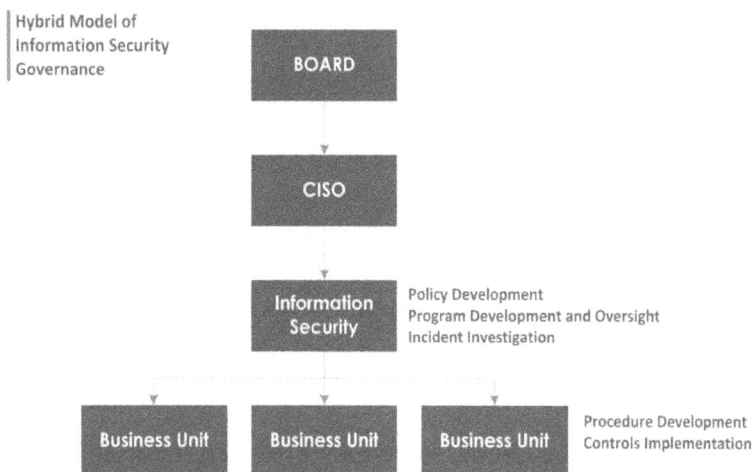

Hybrid Model of Information Security Governance

BOARD

CISO

Information Security — Policy Development / Program Development and Oversight / Incident Investigation

Business Unit   Business Unit   Business Unit — Procedure Development / Controls Implementation

Decentralized Model

In this model, the CISO typically works with a cross-

functional team. The primary advantage of this approach is

that it promotes compliance with information security

standards, as the information security function is positioned

much closer to each business unit. This autonomy allows

the business unit to act in a timelier manner when performing information security functions.

In the decentralized model, each business unit is responsible for its own information security program. Since each one is responsible for developing its own policies and standards, the unit is more likely to comply with the program, assign the necessary resources to it, and fully implement it. Rather than having a generic set of policies that can apply across the organization, this model has the advantage of developing policies aligned with each business unit's particular strategy and business model. Furthermore, the business unit can act autonomously, and thus, theoretically more efficiently when policy changes or incident investigations are necessary.

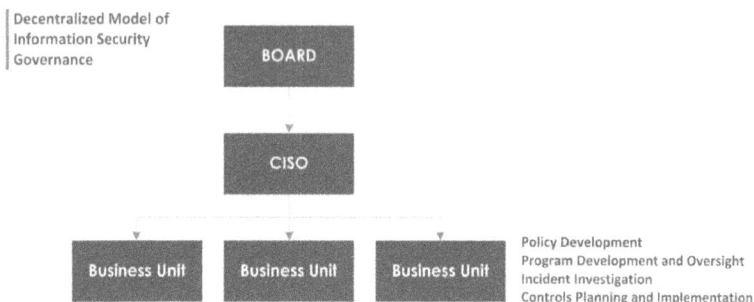

Decentralized Model of Information Security Governance

BOARD

CISO

Business Unit   Business Unit   Business Unit

Policy Development
Program Development and Oversight
Incident Investigation
Controls Planning and Implementation

At the end of the day, information security activities must be coordinated and assigned based on what works best for the organization. Unplanned and uncoordinated localization of authority poses great challenges for institution-wide compliance with security, copyright, privacy, identity and other regulation. It makes it awkward for CISOs to account well for the breadth and depth of overall information security activity, and cause inefficiencies. Localization of authority in some areas might be critical. The question is not to centralize or not to decentralize, but where to centralize (or not) and how to harmonize institutional efforts and investments in information security.

No matter which model an organization chooses to adopt, senior leadership and the Board of Directors must stay involved. Management must communicate clearly that it values and embraces the information security program. The responsible information security group, whether at the corporate level or the business unit level, can only be successful in their initiatives if constituents are held accountable for compliance with the program. Policy violations should be taken very seriously, and must have repercussions. Further, the organization must be willing to be flexible and adjust the program based on feedback and results.

Roles and Responsibilities of the CISO

The typical primary responsibilities of the CISO include the following:

-   *Development and enforcement of security policies, programs, and procedures.* CISOs are responsible for developing and overseeing information security policies, programs, and procedures (depending on the information security governance model within the organization). This involves thinking strategically and tactically, i.e. what the unifying goal of the information security function is, as well as how to execute it. Policies, programs, and procedures must be developed keeping in mind that information assets must be protected, but at the same time, information security controls cannot interfere with core business requirements.

- *Security awareness program.* Users are often seen as a weak point when it comes to security – they can write down their passwords, access files they should not, or leave sensitive customer information lying around. It is, thus, important that they are fully aware of the role they play in security, and are familiar with best practices and guidelines. CISOs are accountable for ensuring that end users are equipped with this knowledge and are able to protect the information assets of the organization. It is important to go to other departments for assistance in educating users. The Learning/Performance Department can help develop tools and courses for users to understand what they can do to maintain security, as well as the rationale behind it.

- ***Incident management and forensics.*** CISOs must ensure that there are systems and controls in place to detect information security incidents. There must also be a standard process for responding to different types of incidents, including root cause analysis, containment, communication, and implementation of any necessary corrective action.

- ***Operational security (includes network and system security management, and application security management).*** CISOs typically develop and supervise their company's network and system infrastructure security policy and standards. They must keep pace with technologies that may be useful to the organization's information security environment or may pose additional risk internally and externally.

Business continuity and disaster recovery. Business

continuity and disaster recovery do are not always the

responsibility of the CISO. Given that availability is an

information security objective however (along with

confidentiality and integrity), business continuity and

disaster recovery functions easily roll up into the CISO's

expanding set of responsibilities. Denial of service attacks,

for example, directly affect systems and information

availability, and fall under information security incident

response. By closely tying business continuity and disaster

recovery to security, it can be ensured that during a security

breach, any forensic evidence is preserved during systems

recovery. Additionally, the CISO can ensure that the

appropriate authorities are notified during or after a breach.

Chapter 3

Cyber Security Readiness

New threats and technologies, including hackers, cybercriminals, smart devices, and the cloud, are all driving how organizations manage their risks and operate in a rapidly changing environment and CISOs must be prepared to manage these challenges. Cyber attacks are growing in sophistication, impact, and volume. The pervasiveness of smart devices, social media, and mobility, further increase the risk of privacy breaches, fraud, and espionage. In today's world, it is not as much a question of *if* but rather *when* an information security breach will occur. This means those organizations, as well as the third parties they do business with, must plan and prepare for how to respond to various scenarios.

Organizations are considering how to manage their risk in fundamentally different ways. By integrating their operations and risk management activities, they can create a smarter and more comprehensive security environment that improves detection, prevention, and response activities in relation to security threats. We can slice information security into these three distinct phases (prevention, detection, and response). CISOs must integrate all three phases of information security to secure information systems and assets. To better illustrate this, suppose the organization had a Class TRTL-30 safe, i.e. a combination-locked safe offering 30 minutes of protection against mechanical, electrical, and cutting tools. The prevention aspect would be its ability to withstand 30 minutes of contact from tools such as cutting wheels, power saws, and

picking tools. After 30 minutes though, without any form

of detection or response, the intruder would be able to

break into the safe and make his escape. On the other hand,

incorporating detection measures (such as an alarm going

off) would alert individuals and allow them to respond

quickly.

Information Security Phases: Prevention, Detection, and Response.

Response feeds lessons learned into prevention, which may require adjustments to prevention measures

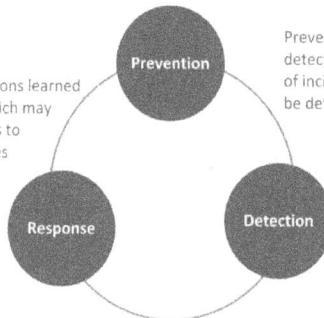

Prevention

Prevention facilitates improved detection and reduces the number of incidents that would otherwise be detected

Response

Detection

Detection drives response and recovery efforts and allows for timely action

Prevention. Security measures must be taken to protect

information from unauthorized modification, destruction,

or disclosure whether accidental or intentional. Information security professionals must continuously develop their capabilities by working smarter, not harder. It is always better to prevent than to have to directly resolve an incident. Prevention includes securing the organization and its information assets with tools, patches, controls, processes, and policies in a timely manner. Furthermore, there must be awareness and education coupled with the reinforcement of good behavior.

Detection. Given the changing threat environment and the limited amount of resources, no system can ever be completely protected. There is no foolproof security solution. It is, thus, important for CISOs to implement a layered defense strategy, in which an alarm is triggered when a layer fails. Intrusion detection systems (IDS) are utilized for this purpose for monitoring system activity and notifying responsible groups or individuals when activities warrant investigation. IDS must have the ability to distinguish normal system activity from malicious activity, which requires some level of fine-tuning to consider known threats, potential intruders, and their methods, etc.

Response. For the detection process to have any value, there must be a timely response, which includes the efficient management of activities to contain, repair, and recover as needed to return to normal business operations. Making important decisions or developing policy while under attack is a recipe for disaster. Many organizations spend a considerable amount of resources preparing for disasters such as tornados, earthquakes, fires, and floods. Resources should similarly be allocated to develop a security incident response plan. The response plan should be approved by appropriate levels of management, and should clearly prioritize different types of events and require a level of notification and/or response suitable for the level of event/threat.

CISOs must pivot organizations to be more proactive in their ability to detect and respond to threats. This means developing cyber analytics and cyber forensics for the purpose of identifying emerging patterns to anticipate intrusions and to track where attacks originate. These foundations of a cyber intelligence framework not only help an organization continuously monitor its risks, but also create a more dynamic situational awareness to drive improved decision-making.

As an additional note, cyber security is supported by both prevention and resilience. Since no organization can protect against every single attack, it is critical to be able to respond and recover from one. Organizations should incorporate resiliency measures into their existing crisis response plans so that senior leaders can communicate them to all stakeholders. Additionally, organizations can train their employees more effectively, especially those with different roles and levels of access.

Vulnerability Management

For all organizations, security is vital, as it not only protects the organization as a whole, but also protects the users and information within it, and the customers and third parties that interact with the organization. In addition, the legal and regulatory requirements should demonstrate all reasonable care in relation to data protection and security. Although information security breaches can never be completely avoided, when it does happen, organizations need to show that they have taken all reasonable steps to mitigate the risk. Vulnerability management is an important part of that process and CISOs must be well equipped to manage vulnerabilities from identification to remedy and follow-up.

System vulnerabilities pose an ongoing challenge for information security, given the continual need to manage vulnerabilities as they are identified in applications, operating systems, hardware configurations, and other technology components. Although some of the common known vulnerabilities discovered in software and systems result from errors introduced during programming, many more come about more innocently, perhaps as a result of poor or unintended system configurations, authorized changes made to enable certain functionalities, or issues that are addressed elsewhere in the environment. Vulnerabilities can even come about from a combination of certain circumstances or software configurations within one environment.

Given the wide range of vulnerabilities that exist or that can arise within an environment, vulnerability management has become a vital part of information security to aid in identifying, classifying, and remediating vulnerabilities. It provides organizations with the ability to evaluate and secure multi-platform and multi-device environments. Using vulnerability management tools, security professionals can map out the state of vulnerability of the organization, using it not only as a guide to target areas of risk, but also to develop policy to mitigate the impact of the threats, and to prevent the accidental creation of vulnerabilities. It, also, is critical to attaining risk management goals as it provides the policy and compliance context, and searches the network for vulnerability information, remediation opportunities, and ultimately, a comprehensive view of enterprise risk. Vulnerability management programs also facilitate compliance with specific regulations that have key security-related aspects, such as the Gramm-Leach-Bliley Act. Effective threat and vulnerability management programs help enterprises meet and exceed these critical compliance requirements.

Threat and vulnerability management programs include three major elements:

1) An information asset inventory,

2) Threat and vulnerability analysis, and

3) Vulnerability management.

Each of these components individually benefits the organization in various ways, but together they form part of an effective threat and vulnerability management program.

Information asset inventory and data classification. To protect information, it is essential that CISOs first know where it resides, as well as its nature and value. Data classification allows for the application of controls that are commensurate with the value of the data, and the impact and probability of associated risks. This understanding will facilitate prioritizing data sets to which more resources should be allocated. For instance, more controls should be implemented around data that is considered customer-sensitive as distinguished from publicly available data.

The information asset inventory must include the physical and logical elements of the information infrastructure, the location, related business processes, data classification, and identified threats and risks for each data element. The physical elements of the information asset inventory include the location equipment such as servers, routers, and storage solutions; paper documents; and related physical storage devices. The logical elements of the asset inventory include the organization's electronic information assets, such as operating systems, and applications. This inventory should also include the primary characteristics of the information that needs to be protected, such as the type and sensitivity of the information and any other critical data points the organization has identified for its information.

The information asset inventory should be readily available to the organization's information security personnel, as well as to the data owners, internal auditors, operations staff, and any other individuals who access that information. To ensure accuracy and completeness of the information asset inventory, the change management process should integrate in into its maintenance. This ensures that the inventory is current and will initiate threat analysis activity if it is based on the characteristics of the data, or whether its use, storage or maintenance has fallen short of specified information security criteria.

Threat and vulnerability Analysis. Threat and vulnerability analysis is an activity that models a certain solution or business process against attack scenarios and vulnerabilities to gauge its resiliency. Some key considerations include the scope of the solution or business process, its value to the organization, any regulatory and legal constraints, as well as the impact on third-party activities. CISOs should be effective in gathering this information through independent discussions with senior managers, consultations with regulators, and interactions with third parties in order to thoroughly evaluate the organization threat and vulnerability posture. Additional information can also be gleaned from the organization's business continuity and disaster recovery plans, which should include this type of information, at least for the critical business processes of the organization.

Vulnerability management uses input from the threat and vulnerability analysis to reduce the risk posed by the identified threats and vulnerabilities. A vulnerability management program consists of four key elements:

- Countermeasure plans with prescriptive guidance on how an organization can repel an attack. The operations staff, which is considered the first line of defense in an attack, should be able to use this to eliminate, or greatly mitigate, the impact of an active attack. A primary benefit of an effective countermeasure plan is how it facilitates assigning the appropriate level of resources required to respond. Purely reactive organizations too often will overreact and over-deploy resources and capabilities in an attempt to counter the attack as quickly as possible. This approach is extremely inefficient and can have significant financial consequences. A sound countermeasure plan can prevent expensive overreaction.

- Once vulnerabilities have been identified, controls should be implanted to address associated risks.

- Metrics and measures provide empirical data to enable an organization to gauge the effectiveness and capability of the threat and vulnerability management analysis as well as the resulting implemented controls.

- Intelligence is a key factor in the threat and vulnerability management program, involving the collection and analysis of data to help distinguish between reality and fear, and uncertainty and doubt. Intelligence can significantly improve the organization's accuracy in threat analysis and vulnerability management activities. It is important to explore all possible scenarios in which an attacker can exploit a business process or a solution, as well as to decide which scenarios are possible in the current state. All this information can be used to modify the security posture and control framework of the organization to defend itself more effectively and efficiently.

Penetration Testing

With multi-tier network architectures, customized applications, and heterogeneous server platform environments, securing data and information assets is more challenging than ever. Although there are various methods and controls to secure systems and applications, the only way to evaluate how secure an organization is to test it, therefore CISOs must not be gun-shy in leveraging third parties or performing management testing of the internal network. By having penetration tests performed against the environment, CISOs can simulate the actions that a malicious attacker would take, providing a more accurate representation of the security posture at a given point in time. Penetration testing benefits the organization.

Finding vulnerabilities before they are exploited. At any given time, attackers are employing tools and methods looking for ways to penetrate systems. Only a handful of those attackers will have access to actual exploits, and most of them will be using well known, and thus, preventable, attacks and exploits. Penetration testing provides IT and security with a view of their network from a malicious point of view. By having an external group analyze in an attempt to find ways into networks, creates a much better position to fix these holes before someone with malicious intentions discovers them.

Reporting problems to senior management. If the CISO has already reported to upper management certain weaknesses within the environment, penetration-testing results help to justify the resources necessary to address those weaknesses. By having an external group with security expertise analyze a system or systems, management will often be more agreeable to allocating more resources to security, particularly since an external tester has no vested interest in their results.

Similarly, system administrators who know the intricacies of their environment are often aware of how to compromise their network. It is not uncommon for management to assume that without such knowledge, an attacker would be unable to gain unauthorized entry. By using an external group who has no inside knowledge, the penetration testing team may be able to identify the same vulnerabilities and help convince management that they need to be addressed.

Validating secure configurations. The penetration test report verifies that the CISO and security staff is effectively securing the organization. Having an external entity verify security provides an objective view devoid of internal preferences. The penetration test does not directly improve security, but it does identify gaps between knowledge and implementation. The approach of validating secure configurations gives visibility into the vulnerabilities that could be exploited further increasing the risk of compromise. Therefore, CISOs should pay very close attention to the details in configuration settings and ensure consistent application of configurations throughout the organization.

Evaluating potential training needs for IT and security staff. Penetration testing gives IT and the security staff a chance to recognize and respond to a network attack. If the penetration tester were to successfully compromise a system without detection, this could indicate a failure to adequately train staff on security monitoring. Testing the monitoring and incident response teams can verify if they are able to detect what is going on and measure the effectiveness of their response.

Identifying gaps in compliance. Penetration testers often breach a perimeter because not all the machines were patched or possibly because a non-compliant machine was temporarily set up and ended up becoming a critical resource. In this heavily regulated environment, many organizations are looking for better ways to continually evaluate their compliance posture.

As for compliance with laws and regulations, some organizations are subject to requirements (such as the Payment Card Industry Data Security Standard, or PCI-DSS) mandating that penetration testing be performed.

Testing new technology prior to rollout. The best time to test new technology is before it is rolled out into production. Performing a penetration test on new technologies, applications, and environments before they go into production can often save time and money because it is easier to test and modify new technology while nobody is relying on it.

Security Monitoring

Today's environment constantly poses new risks, yet countermeasures and technologies such as intrusion detection systems, anti-virus software, or log-aggregation tools fail to provide the visibility into the environment that is necessary. To cope with the multitude of risks, it is essential to know what is happening across the network at all times, and the response must be immediate, armed with pervasive and actionable intelligence, and up-to-date situational awareness. CISOs must engage in active monitoring of assets and information flows.

For most organizations, network monitoring tools are a well-established part of IT operations, serving the role of letting the IT shop know when service quality is impacted, such as when network connections are down or underperforming, or when key resources such as critical servers or applications are non-functional. Rarely, though, are they used in a focused manner by the security team.

Probably the most direct area where network monitoring tools can add security value is in denial of service (DoS) conditions (including distributed denial of service or DDoS attacks). The DDoS attacks on the financial industry that began in late 2012 (claimed by a group called the Izz ad-Din al-Qassam Cyber Fighters) intended to disrupt consumer online banking services. The main consequence was user frustration and a negative impact on the reputation of the attacked banks. An NBC News report[11] found that in the six weeks prior, 15 of the nation's largest banks were offline for a total of 249 hours due to these cyber attacks. Banks that were attacked include Capital One Financial Corp., Wells Fargo, JP Morgan, and Bank of America, among others. DoS conditions, whether

---

[11] "Cyber attacks on banks signal urgent need for security bill, lawmakers say." NBC News. Retrieved from http://www.nbcnews.com/technology/cyberattacks-banks-signal-urgent-need-security-bill-lawmakers-say-1C9202532.

caused deliberately and maliciously or accidentally, share one key characteristic – unavailability of resources. One of the primary uses for network monitoring tools is monitoring for this type of condition.

Incident investigation support is another area where network monitoring tools can be useful. In the same way that network monitoring tools provide early warning of DoS attacks, these tools also can assist in incident investigation as they provide information on patterns of activity that could result from a security event. Many of the attack techniques that intruders employ to enter systems can result in services or hosts becoming temporarily unavailable. For example, many buffer overflow conditions, when exploited, will cause services to become unresponsive or, in extreme cases, trigger system termination and subsequent restart.

Thresholds are a part of monitoring and should be formally established and documented. Establishing a practical threshold that can be easily defined and accurately measured, and subsequently alerting when the threshold is crossed is a fundamental part of monitoring.

Incident and Problem Management

In 2006, a government laptop stolen from the home of a Veteran Affairs data analyst contained Social Security numbers and other personal information for over 26 million veterans and active duty troops. A class action suit brought by veterans groups was settled by the agency in the value of $20 million.

In 2008, 134 million credit cards were exposed through SQL injection to install spyware on Heartland Payment Systems' data systems. The vulnerability to SQL injection was well understood, and security analysts had warned retailers about it for several years. Yet, the continuing vulnerability of many Internet-facing applications made SQL injection the most common form of attack against websites at that time.

Also in 2008, a flash drive infected with malicious code was plugged into a military laptop at a base in the Middle East, resulting in "the most significant breach of US military computers ever," according to William J. Lynn III, then-deputy secretary of Defense. The code invaded a network run by US Central Command and established a point from which data could be transferred to servers under foreign control.

In 2012, the South Carolina Department of Revenue's website from late-August to mid-October was hacked at least five times. The intruders took 3.6 million Social Security numbers and 387,000 payment card records.

While the vast majority of the credit card numbers were encrypted, none of the Social Security numbers was.

Internet hacking of government networks is nothing new. There have been over 600 publicly disclosed cases of breaches of government and military networks since 2005, in which at least 141 million records were stolen.[12]

In light of these examples, incident and problem management take center stage and CISOs need to take heed and be vigilant in implementing strong, easily to follow incident management processes. First, it is important to make the distinction between an incident and a problem in order to understand the distinction between incident management and problem management. An incident is "an event which is not part of the standard operation of a service and which causes or may cause disruption to or a

---

[12] The Privacy Rights Clearinghouse Chronology of Data Breaches. Retrieved from http://www.privacyrights.org/data-breach.

reduction in the quality of services and customer productivity."[13] A problem, on the other hand, is "the unknown root cause of one or more existing or potential Incidents. Problems may sometimes be identified because of multiple incidents that exhibit common symptoms. Problems can also be identified from a single significant incident, indicative of a single error, for which the cause is unknown. Occasionally problems will be identified well before any related incidents occur."[13]

The primary goal of incident management is to restore normal service operations as quickly as possible as well as to minimize the impact on business operations, therefore ensuring that the best possible levels of service quality and availability are maintained. Problem management, by contrast, includes the activities required to diagnose

---

[13] Information Technology Infrastructure Library Version 2. Retrieved from http://www.itil-officialsite.com.

the root cause of the incidents and to determine the resolution to the problem. It is also tied to ensuring that the resolution is implemented through the appropriate control procedures, specifically change management and release management. The primary objectives of problem management are as follows:

- To ensure there is traceability and accountability of actions
- To offer management insights into the operational effectiveness of controls
- To prevent problems and resulting incidents from happening
- To have a consistent approach towards resolving incidents and problems
- To protect organizations from liability

- To reduce the risk of problems escalating to a major crisis

Problem management works with incident management and change management to ensure service availability and quality. Upon incident resolution, information about the resolution is recorded. Over time, this information is used to speed up the resolution time and identify permanent solutions, reducing the volume and resolution time of incidents. This results in reduced downtime and reduced disruption to business-critical systems.

Developing an Effective Incident and Problem Management Program

A strong incident and problem management program is based on investigations and intelligence, and detection and response.

Investigations and Intelligence aid in the prevention of incidents, including cyber attacks, internal malicious users, unsuspecting users aiding criminals and cyber attackers and bi-directional attacks, and so on. Given this wide range of potential points of attack, a CISO needs to be aware of internal and external factors that influence the organization using investigation and intelligence.

- *Cross-Functional Intelligence.* Coordination with other groups such as human resources and legal departments. For example, knowledge of disgruntled employees might be useful in incident investigation and management. Monitoring systems can be leveraged to understand user behavior.

- *Deep Web and Darknet.* Sometimes taking a look into the dark side of the Internet gives CISOs insight into whether their organizations are part of the Internet "black market." The deep web refers to content that is not indexed by standard search engines. Darknets are distinct from other distributed P2P networks in that information sharing is anonymous – users, whether governmental or corporate, thus, can communicate with little fear of interference. Occasionally, there will be chatter about certain organizations in these underground channels. It is useful to plug into these sources for intelligence and investigation purposes.

Detection and Response is what comes after an organization has been penetrated and it is there that traceability is necessary and an incident response plan needs to, to be prepared; an incident response team needs to be defined and ready to go, drills should have been conducted so members of such team know what they need to know during an incident and can react quickly.

Organization

Centralized or Hybrid Model

In a centralized or hybrid approach, incident and problem management is performed by the security group. Incidents may be detected by the security group as they perform systems monitoring, or may be reported by IT or end users. The security group is responsible for investigating the incident, determining the business impact and extent of the incident, and taking corrective action. The ISG works with entities such as the business unit and IT during this process. Any information security incidents are sent up to the CISO as appropriate.

Decentralized Model

In a decentralized model, incident and problem management is performed by IT. Incidents may be detected by IT as they perform systems monitoring, or may be reported by users within the business unit. IT is then responsible for investigating the incident, determining the

business impact and extent of the incident, and taking

corrective action. Any information security incidents are

escalated to the CISO as appropriate.

Security Architecture

All too often, IT projects are designed to address the

core business requirements without much consideration for

the security of the solution. Consequently, security is often

only an afterthought and included only during the last

stages of project design, which could result in security

weaknesses, therefore CISOs need a sound business-IT

strategy to engage with the business and form the right

coalitions to ensure that security is built into the design

phase of projects. As organizations evolve their IT

architectures, they must ensure that the corresponding

security controls remain up to date and capable of addressing constantly changing security threats, including external issues such as cyber security.

Security architecture and engineering focuses on the alignment of the organization's security processes and systems with business goals and information security policies. It facilitates traceability from the business strategy down to the underlying technology. Primary functions within this area include ensuring integration of IT systems development with information security policies and strategies; developing and maintaining information security policies and standards related to encryption, intrusion detection, and network authentication; and providing technical guidance to business units on risk mitigation. A strong enterprise information security architecture process helps to answer basic questions such as:

- What is the security risk posture of the organization?
- Does the current environment support and add value to the organization?
- How might the current environment be modified so that it adds more value to the organization?
- Will the current environment support near-term or long-term goals of the business?

Security architecture is a critical facet of the CISO's role, especially since a host of security issues can exist at the application layer. Although CISOs and security professionals are not expected to know how to write code, they should be familiar with the potential security issues around software. Addressing these issues should be incorporated into application development activities, and developers should be trained to create solutions based on security principles established by initiatives such as the

Open Web Application Security Project (OWASP) and

entities such as SANS. Although it is not possible to

completely eliminate all risk at the application layer,

keeping these principles in mind make for good

architecture and engineering.

As an organization's IT infrastructure becomes

increasingly complex and interconnected, the difficulty of

achieving application security increases correspondingly.

Organizations can no longer afford to tolerate relatively

simple security problems such as those presented in the

OWASP Top 10,[14] which identifies some of the most

critical application security risks facing organizations and

is referenced by various resources and organizations such

as PCI-DSS, MITRE, and the Defense Information Systems

---

[14] OWASP. (2013). OWASP Top 10 List. Retrieved from
https://www.owasp.org/index.php/Top_10_2013-T10.

Agency (DISA). Examples of security issues on the list are as follows:

- Injection flaws, such as SQL, OS, and LDAP injection occur when untrusted data is sent to an interpreter as part of a command or query. The attacker's hostile data can trick the interpreter into executing unintended commands or accessing unauthorized data.

- Application functions related to authentication and session management are often not implemented correctly, allowing attackers to compromise passwords, keys, session tokens, or exploit other implementation flaws to assume other users' identities.

- A direct object reference occurs when a developer exposes a reference to an internal implementation object such as a file, directory, or database key. Without an access control check or other protection, attackers can manipulate these references to access unauthorized data.

- Many web applications do not properly protect sensitive data, such as credit cards; tax IDs, and authentication credentials. Attackers may steal or modify such weakly protected data to conduct identity theft, credit card fraud, or other crimes. Sensitive data deserves extra protection such as encryption at rest or in transit, as well as special precautions when exchanged with the browser.

Another listing of risky software errors is the *SANS Top 25 Most Dangerous Software Errors*,[15] which identifies the

---

[15] MITRE. (2011). SANS Top 25 Most Dangerous Software Errors. Retrieved from http://cwe.mitre.org/top25/archive/2011/2011_cwe_sans_top25.pdf.

most widespread and critical errors that can lead to serious vulnerabilities in software. They are dangerous because they will frequently allow attackers to completely take over the software, steal data, or prevent the software from working at all. The software errors have been classified into three high-level categories:

Insecure interaction between components. These weaknesses are related to insecure ways in which data is sent and received between separate components, modules, programs, processes, threads, or systems.

- Improper neutralization of special elements used in an SQL command (SQL Injection)
- Improper neutralization of input during web page generation (cross-site scripting)
- Unrestricted upload of file with dangerous type
- URL redirection to an untrusted site (open redirect)

Risky resource management. The weaknesses in this category are related to ways in which software does not properly manage the creation, usage, transfer, or destruction of important system resources.

- Buffer copy without checking size of input (classic buffer overflow)

- Improper limitation of a pathname to a restricted directory (path traversal)

- Download of code without an integrity check

Porous defenses. The weaknesses in this category are related to defensive techniques that are often misused, abused, or just plain ignored.

- Missing authentication for critical function

- Missing authorization

- Use of hard-coded credentials

- Missing encryption of sensitive data

Aside from being familiar with common risky application security weaknesses, it is also important for CISOs to consider the security of applications offered by software vendors. When selecting a vendor for software, CISOs should be embedded in the procurement and contract negotiation process. CISOs must have a baseline set of security standards agreed to by the business beforehand that goes into the software procurement request. These standards should cover access management, audit and logging, monitoring, etc. Aside from the obvious benefit of aligning the vendor's security practices with that of the organization, this approach tells the vendor that the organization is serious about security, and that the software must meet a certain standard to be part of the organization's portfolio. These baseline standards can also be used in the vendor selection process, i.e. if the software doesn't meet the standards, the organization will not do business with them. The CISO works with the Legal and Procurement departments on standard language to be included in contracts and master services agreements. It is important to note that external reports of software controls, such as Statements on Standards for Attestation Engagements (SSAE No. 16) or Service Organization Controls (SOC) reports (which have replaced the now-obsolete Statement on Auditing Standards No. 70 or SAS 70 reports) and other third party audit reports provided by the vendor should be given more weight relative to security questionnaires they have filled out themselves.

Third Party Security Management

Today's business environment is increasingly dependent on third party relationships as organizations focus on their core competencies and outsource many non-core activities. Such outsourcing is justified by savings based on cost, competencies, or effort of performance in-house. In turn, the heightened security expected by customers coupled with a growing emphasis on legal and regulatory compliance requires evidence of adequate governance measures. When internal functions such as information technology, human resources, payroll processing, or other services are outsourced to third parties, the risks to information confidentiality, integrity, and availability can be very significant. It is important to recognize that many regulations make no distinction in responsibilities between the target organization and its outsourcing providers. Thus, the twin issues of due diligence and ongoing oversight over third parties have become vital to CISOs in establishing and maintaining relationships with third parties.

Initial due diligence. This refers to the initial activities that must be performed prior to formalizing a relationship with a third party. Once the current status is documented, the findings are used to develop a plan for mitigating any significant risks where possible.

- Review existing general security practices of the third party, as well as other areas as applicable (such as financial viability, compliance practices, technology compatibility and security, etc.)

- Perform a gap analysis between existing and recommended practices

- Create and implement a plan for mitigating significant risks, whether by additional internal controls, contract terms, etc.

Ongoing third party oversight. The oversight or
monitoring component of third party governance implies
that the third party will be subject to review and evaluation
of its performance over time. This must be exercised for all
risk aspects of the relationship, whether business, security
or information technology, on a regular basis. Key points to
consider in this component are as follows:

- Establish a scheduled review cycle for all third
  party security relationships, with the frequency
  dependent on the level of risk posed by the third
  party

- Use metrics (within the context of service level
  agreements) to measure the third party's functional
  performance and improve performance as needed

- Evaluate the relevant risk aspects of the relationship
  to identify any significant changes in the risk profile

of the third party (and if there are any, mitigate risk where possible)

Information Security Awareness and Training

It is generally understood by security professionals that people are one of the weakest links in the effort to secure systems and networks, yet at the same time, people are key to providing an adequate and appropriate level of security. In other words, security is as much a human issue as it is a technology issue. A robust and enterprise-wide awareness and training program is thus paramount to ensuring that people understand their security responsibilities, organizational policies, and how to properly use and protect the information assets entrusted to them. Security awareness and training should be focused on the organization's entire user population, including senior and executive managers.

To establish the foundation for success in awareness and training, CISO's must first, distinguish between awareness and training must be distinguished to ensure that both are addressed holistically in learning about security. Awareness is defined as follows:

> The purpose of awareness presentations is simply to focus attention on security. Awareness presentations are intended to allow individuals to recognize IT security concerns and respond accordingly. In awareness activities, the learner is the recipient of information, whereas the learner in a training environment has a more active role. Awareness relies on reaching broad audiences with attractive packaging techniques. Training is more formal, having a goal of building knowledge and skills to facilitate the job performance.[16]

---

[16] De Zafra, E.; Pitcher, S.; Tressler, J.; Ippolito, J. (1998). *Information Technology Security Training Requirements* (NIST Special Publication 800-16). Retrieved from http://csrc.nist.gov/publications/nistpubs/800-16/800-16.pdf.

An example of a topic for an awareness session or awareness material is virus protection, and would cover what a virus is, what could happen if a virus infects a system, what the user should do to prevent infection, and what the user should upon discovery.

Training, by contrast, is defined as:

> The 'Training' level of the learning continuum strives to produce relevant and needed security skills and competencies by practitioners of functional specialties other than IT security (e.g., management, systems design and development, acquisition, auditing).[17]

The most significant difference between training and awareness is that training aims to teach skills, which allow a person to perform a specific function, while awareness

---

[17] De Zafra, E.; Pitcher, S.; Tressler, J.; Ippolito, J. (1998). *Information Technology Security Training Requirements* (NIST Special Publication 800-16). Retrieved from http://csrc.nist.gov/publications/nistpubs/800-16/800-16.pdf.

seeks to focus attention on an issue. The skills acquired during training are built upon the foundation of awareness. An example of training is an IT security course for system administrators, which should address in detail the management, operational and technical controls that should be implemented.

An awareness and training program is crucial in that it is the vehicle for conveying information that users need in order to do their jobs in a secure manner, based on security requirements within the organization. The program should communicate key security policies and procedures, building the basis for any sanctions due to noncompliance. Accountability is derived from a fully informed, well-trained, and aware workforce.

A strong security program cannot be implemented fully without awareness of and education on security processes.

In addition, those in the organization who manage the IT infrastructure and security functions need to have the skills necessary to perform their assigned duties effectively.

Organizations cannot protect the confidentiality, integrity, and availability of information assets without ensuring that its people:

- Understand their roles and responsibilities related to the organizational mission

- Understand the organization's security policy, procedures, and practices

- Have adequate knowledge of the various management, operational, and technical controls required and available to protect the IT resources for which they are responsible

Organization

Centralized Model

In a centralized model, all responsibility resides with a central authority (i.e., CISO and security department). All directives, strategy development, planning, and scheduling is coordinated through this authority. Because the awareness and training strategy is developed by the central authority, the needs assessment is also conducted by the central authority. The central authority also develops the training plan and materials. The methods for implementing the material throughout the organization is determined and accomplished by the central authority.

The central authority communicates the organization's policy directives regarding security awareness and training, the strategy for conducting the program, and the material and method of delivery. The business units provide information requested by the central authority, including providing feedback on the effectiveness of awareness and training materials. This allows the central authority to fine-tune, add or delete material, or modify the delivery methods.

Hybrid Model

In this model, security awareness and training policy and strategy are defined by a central authority, but implementation is delegated to business unit managers. Awareness and training budget allocation, material development, and scheduling are the responsibilities of these managers.

The needs assessment is conducted by the central authority, because it still determines the strategy for the awareness and training program. Policy, strategy, and budget are passed from the central authority to the organizational units. Based on the strategy, the organizational units then develop their own training plans and materials.

The central authority may advise the business units that they are responsible for developing training plans and for implementing the program, and may provide guidance or training to the organizational units so that they can perform their responsibilities.

Decentralized Model

In this model, the central security awareness and training authority distributes broad policy and expectations regarding security awareness and training requirements, but extends responsibility for executing the entire program down to the business units. This model normally uses a series of distributed authority directives, mandated by the central authority.

The needs assessment is conducted by each business unit, because the units determine the strategy for the awareness and training program. Based on the strategy, the organizational units develop their own training plans and materials.

The central authority may also advise the organizational units that they are responsible for conducting their own needs assessment, developing their strategy, developing training plans, and implementing the program, and may provide guidance or training to the organizational units so that they can carry out their responsibilities

Given the distribution of responsibilities, the central authority may require periodic input from each business unit, reporting the budget expenditures made, the status and results of needs assessments, the strategy chosen by the business unit, the status of training plans, and progress

reports on the implementation of the awareness and training
material.

Information Security Reporting and Metrics

An activity cannot be managed effectively if it cannot be

measured and CISOs need to be able to measure their

effectiveness to the organization and provide useful metrics

to upper management for making decisions. Information

security metrics indicate the effectiveness of existing

controls in relation to policy objectives, whether the scope

is a specific component of the security programs, a specific

system, product or process, or the ability of departments

within an organization to respond to security issues for

which they are responsible. These metrics can be obtained

at different levels within the organization, i.e. collected at

the system and network level, and subsequently aggregated

and summarized for reporting to management. Metrics can also provide guidance in prioritizing corrective actions. Finally, with the knowledge gained through metrics, security managers can gain a historical view of the organization's level of security and quantify improvements in the security posture through time, as well as compare security against industry benchmarks and other companies within the same and other industries.

Examples of key metrics that may be provided are as follows:

- Baseline defenses coverage, including antivirus, antispyware, and firewalls, can be expressed as percentage of devices covered, average number of days since last update, etc.

- Patch latency, or the time between the release of a patch and the organization's deployment of the patch

- Platform compliance scores

- Number and types of suspected and actual access violations

- Number and types of malicious code incidents prevented

- Number and types of security incidents

Organization

Centralized or Hybrid Model

In a centralized or hybrid approach to information security metrics, the CISO is responsible for communicating information security metrics and risk assessment results, along with any recommendations, to the board in an annual report. This report is a summary of risk assessment findings and recommendations; action plans for implementation, and key performance measures to indicate progress towards information security objectives.

Metrics are obtained from IT and/or the security department, for submission to the CISO for review and approval. The internal audit group may request for copies of these reports for monitoring and tracking purposes. The security department will then work with the internal audit group to address any findings.

Decentralized Model

Similar to the centralized or hybrid model, in a decentralized model, the CISO is responsible for reporting information security metrics and risk assessment results, along with any recommendations, to the board. Metrics are obtained from IT and business units. The internal audit group would then work with the IT department to address any findings.

Business Continuity and Disaster Recovery

As organizations become increasingly dependent on technology and real-time, business-critical information, protecting information assets and providing for their continuity and recovery becomes an even greater priority. The importance of protecting irreplaceable data cannot be emphasized enough. Despite best efforts and precautions, disasters and crises eventually strike an organization. Natural disasters such as earthquakes and hurricanes, as well as other events like building fires and defective plumbing, can pose significant threats to an organization. Every organization is at risk from potential disasters that include:

- Natural disasters such as tornadoes, floods, blizzards, and earthquakes

- Accidents

- Power and energy disruptions

- Communications and transportation sector failure

- Environmental disasters

- Cyber attacks and hacker activity

Well-prepared organizations establish plans and procedures in order to reduce the impact any form of disaster may have on continuing business operations and to help facilitate a speedy recovery. The CISO's focus on availability is paramount, particularly since attacks using a DoS approach are becoming more and more frequent.

Business continuity and disaster recovery planning consists of four major components: 1) identifying risks and analyzing business impacts, 2) designing the strategy, 3) developing and executing plans, and 4) testing and maintaining plans.

Identifying risks and creating a business impact analysis is crucial to this function as it provides an overview of the internal and external forces that pose risks to the organization. By establishing this organizational risk profile, we can prioritize which risks to address first and how to address them (i.e., mitigate, transfer, or accept).

The business continuity strategy must be consistent with business objectives and the risk appetite of the organization. Will a conservative approach be more acceptable? Will there be enough resources for the strategy being considered? How much risk is the organization willing to take on? These are some questions that are answered during this stage.

Establishing a business continuity plan consistent with the organization's strategy helps ensure that resources and structures are in place to deal with these emergency situations. Critical services or products are those that must be delivered to ensure survival, avoid causing injury, and meet legal, regulatory, or other obligations of an organization. Business continuity planning is a proactive process that ensures critical products and services are delivered during a business interruption or disruption. A business continuity plan includes:

- Plans, measures, and procedures to ensure the continuous operation of critical services and products, which allows the company to recover its facility, information, and assets

- Identification of necessary resources to support business continuity, including employees, information assets, equipment, budgeting, legal

counsel, infrastructure protection, etc.

Having a business continuity plan enhances an

organization's image among the shareholders and

customers by demonstrating a proactive attitude. Additional

benefits include the improvement in overall organizational

efficiency and identifying the relationship between assets

and human and financial resources and critical services and

deliverables. These plans must be tested periodically and

updated as needed.

Disaster Recovery Strategies
Cold Sites

The cold site is the barebones approach to disaster

recovery. These facilities have the basic equipment needed

to run a data center, such as HVAC, power and network

connectivity, but not much more than that. Cold sites

provide coverage for long-term outages of the primary site, such as those caused by a building fire, hurricane, or other major disaster that render the primary site completely inoperable. If a disaster does occur, an organization must then acquire the hardware necessary to resume operations, build systems, install applications, and load data from backup tapes. Recovery time for cold sites is measured in days or weeks rather than in hours – there is always this tradeoff between cost and recovery time with any disaster recovery approach.

Warm Sites

For many businesses, the long activation time required getting the cold site up and running presents an unacceptable risk. Warm sites address this by going beyond the basic infrastructure at a cold site to include the hardware necessary for operations restoration. Depending on the nature of the warm site, the organization may also choose to have the hardware already loaded with the operating systems and applications required to resume operations.

Warm sites also include a copy of the organization's data in some form. This could be as simple as storing backup tapes at the location and planning to restore all data from tape upon site activation, or it might be more advanced and include systems with replicated copies of the data.[18]

Hot Sites

Hot sites provide instantaneous or near real-time recovery of operations when the primary site fails. Hot sites build upon the warm site concept but take it to the next

---

[18] Chapple, M. (2012). *Which Disaster Recovery Site Strategy Is Right For You?* Retrieved from http://www.biztechmagazine.com/article/2012/06/which-disaster-recovery-site-strategy-right-you.

level by ensuring that systems at the site are preloaded with operating systems, applications, and the data assets necessary to pick up operations. The significant investment of time and money required to set up a hot site provides the organization with the ability to resume operations in minutes or even seconds after a disaster interrupts operations at the primary site.

A hybrid approach may be used as well, striking a balance between a warm site and a hot site. Some organizations that have a handful of critical systems and processes choose to implement a hybrid approach that uses hot site capabilities for a smaller number of critical services and a warm site approach for other systems that have a longer maximum tolerable downtime. This allows disaster recovery planners to focus scarce resources on the most critical processes without completely neglecting other

services.

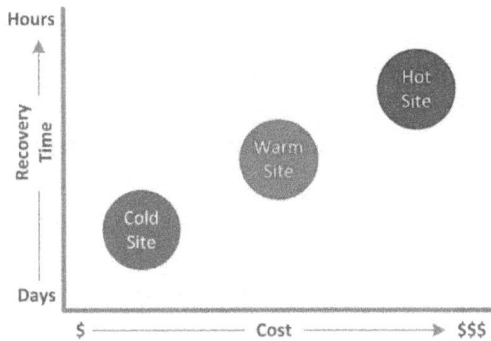

Disaster Recovery Strategies and Corresponding Tradeoffs.

Computer Incident Response Team (CIRT)

Attacks on information systems have increased in

both number and sophistication in recent years. While

preventing such attacks would be less costly and would be

the ideal scenario for any organization, not all incidents can

be prevented. Risks can never be completely averted or

eliminated. Organizations should empower CISOs to

identify and evaluate the risks to its information assets, and mitigate those risks to an acceptable level and CISOs should manage up to ensure that organization leadership understands the value of establishing a Computer Incident Response Team.

A key element of this risk management process is the analysis of previous incidents, identifying trends and effective responses. A well-defined incident response capability helps the organization detect incidents rapidly, minimize loss and destruction, identify weaknesses and inadequate controls, and quickly restore IT operations.[19]

It can be difficult to maintain situational awareness in responding to significant, high-impact incidents because of their scale and complexity. Additionally, coordinating incident handling activities between different groups with

---

[19] Bowen, P.; Hash, J.; Wilson, M. (2006). *Information Security Handbook* (NIST Special Publication 800-100). Retrieved from http://csrc.nist.gov/publications/nistpubs/800-100/SP800-100-Mar07-2007.pdf

different roles throughout the process can be challenging. Many people within the organization may play a role in the incident response, and the organization may need to communicate rapidly and efficiently with various external groups. Collecting and analyzing all the information so that the right decisions can be made and executed are not easy tasks. The key to maintaining situational awareness is to prepare thoroughly, which includes establishing and maintaining notification mechanisms and guidelines for prioritizing incidents, and ensuring that all members of the team are fully-equipped and aware of their role in the process.

The services of Computer Incident Response Teams (CIRTs) can be grouped into three categories. This section focuses on reactive services, which encompasses incident handling, as this is the core component of the CIRT function.[20]

- ***Reactive services.*** These services are triggered by an event or request, such as a report of a compromised system, wide-spreading malicious code, software vulnerability, or something that was identified by an intrusion detection system. Examples of activities under this group are:

  - Incident handling: incident analysis, incident response and support, incident response coordination

  - Vulnerability handling: vulnerability analysis, vulnerability response, vulnerability response coordination

---

[20] West-Brown, M.; Stikvoort, D., et al. (2003). *Handbook for CSIRTs*. Retrieved from http://www.sei.cmu.edu/reports/03hb002.pdf

- Artifact handling: artifact analysis, artifact response, artifact response coordination

- ***Proactive services.*** These services provide assistance and information to help prepare, protect, and secure information systems in anticipation of attacks, problems, or events. Performance of these services on an ongoing basis will directly reduce the number of incidents in the future. Examples of specific services in this area are as follows:

  - Security audit or assessments
  - Configuration and maintenance of security tools, applications, etc.
  - Development of security tools
  - Intrusion detection services
  - Security-related information dissemination

- *Security quality management services.* These services extend well-established services that are independent of incident handling and traditionally performed by other areas of an organization such as the IT, audit, or training functions. If the CIRT performs or assists with these services, the CIRT's perspective and expertise can be leveraged to improve the overall security of the organization. This area focuses on activities such as:

  - Risk analysis
  - Business continuity and disaster recovery planning
  - Security consulting
  - Awareness building
  - Education and training

Detection and Analysis

Under the umbrella of reactive services, incident handling involves receiving and responding to incident reports, as well as analyzing those reported or detected incidents and events. Detection and analysis, i.e. accurately determining whether an incident has occurred and, if so, its type, extent, and magnitude are, for many organizations, the more challenging aspects of the incident response process. Two major activities that may be part of incident analysis, depending on the structure and defined roles of the CIRT are as follows:

- *Forensic evidence collection*. This refers to the collection, documentation, and analysis of forensic evidence gathered from a compromised system to determine system changes and to assist in the reconstruction of events leading to the compromise.

This gathering of information must be done in such a way that documents a provable chain of custody that is admissible in a court of law. Tasks involved in forensic evidence collection include, but are not limited to, making a copy of the affected systems' hard drives; checking for changes to the system such as new programs, files, and users; examining processes that are running; and checking for things such as Trojan horse programs and toolkits. CIRT employees performing this function may also have to be prepared to act as expert witnesses in court proceedings.

- *Tracking or tracing*. This sub-service refers to the tracing of the origins and access point of an intruder or identifying systems to which the intruder had access. This involves tracking or tracing how the intruder entered the affected systems and related networks, the systems were used to gain access, the origination point of the attack, and any other systems and networks were used as part of the attack. It might also involve trying to determine the identity of the intruder. This work might be done internally but usually involves working with law enforcement, internet service providers, or other external entities.

Incidents can be detected through various methods, with different levels of detail and reliability. Automated detection capabilities include network-based and host-based intrusion detection systems (IDSs), antivirus software, and log analyzers. Incidents may also be detected through manual means, such as user reports. Some incidents have obvious indicators that can be easily detectable, whereas others are virtually undetectable without automation.

When a potential incident is identified, the incident response team should work quickly to analyze and validate it, documenting each step taken throughout the process. The team should perform an initial analysis to determine the incident's scope; attack methods employed, and targeted vulnerabilities. This analysis should provide enough information for the team to prioritize subsequent activities, including the containment of the incident. Particular response activities can include:

- Taking action to protect systems and networks affected by intruder activity

- Providing solutions and mitigation strategies from relevant advisories or alerts

- Searching for intruder activity on other parts of the network

- Rebuilding systems and patching or repairing systems

- Developing other response or workaround strategies

When in doubt, incident handlers should assume the worst until additional analyses indicate otherwise. In addition to prioritization guidelines, organizations should also establish an escalation process for those instances when the incident response team fails to respond to an incident within the designated time.

Containment, Eradication, and Recovery

It is important to contain an incident before it spreads in order to avoid putting an overwhelming strain on resources and increasing, or poorly managing, damage caused by the incident. Most incidents require containment;

therefore, it is important to evaluate this option early on in the course of handling each incident. An essential part of containment is decision making, such as whether to shut down a system, disconnect it from the network, or disable certain functions. Such decisions are much easier to make if procedures for containing the incident have been predetermined; therefore, it is vital that CISOs ensure that organizations have well documented processes as it relates to incident recovery.

Organizations should define risk thresholds and develop strategies accordingly. With this baseline in place, organizations will have a better grasp of the risk tolerance framework within which they will operate and make decisions.

Containment strategies vary based on the type of incident. For example, the overall strategy for containing an e-mail-borne virus infection would be different from that of

a network-based distributed denial of service attack.

Organizations should create separate and distinct

containment strategies for each major type of incident. The

criteria for choosing the appropriate strategy should be

documented clearly to facilitate quick and effective

decision making to allow for timely action. Examples of

criteria include potential damage to and theft of resources,

the need to properly preserve evidence, the effectiveness of

the strategy, the time and resources needed to implement

the strategy, and the duration of the solution.

After an incident has been contained, eradication

may be necessary to eliminate components or remnants of

the incident, such as deleting malicious code and disabling

breached user accounts. For some incidents, eradication is

either unnecessary or is performed during recovery. In

recovery, system administrators restore systems to normal operations and, if applicable, also harden systems to prevent similar incidents. Recovery may involve such actions as:

- Restoring systems from clean backups and rebuilding them

- Replacing compromised files with clean versions

- Tightening network perimeter security (e.g., firewall rules)

Post-Incident Activity
After a major incident has been handled, the CISO should organize a lessons-learned meeting to review the effectiveness of the incident handling process and identify necessary improvements to existing security controls and practices. Lessons-learned meetings should also be held periodically for smaller incidents. The information

accumulated from all lessons-learned meetings, as well as the data collected while handling each incident, should be used to identify systemic security weaknesses and deficiencies in policies and procedures. Through these discussions, best practices can also be identified and incorporated in existing processes to improve incident handling.

Roles and Responsibilities

A CIRT is a cross-functional, carefully selected and well-trained group of people whose purpose is to promptly and correctly handle an incident so that it can be quickly contained, investigated, and recovered from. It is usually comprised of members from within the company.[21]

---

[21] Borodkin, M. (2001). *Computer Incident Response Team.* Retrieved from http://www.sans.org/reading_room/whitepapers/incident/computer-incident-response-team_641.

	Management	CISO	Security	IT	Audit	Legal	HR	Public Relations
Detection and Analysis	I	A	R	R				C
Investigation and Forensics	I	A	R	R		C		C
Recovery	I	A	R	R		C		C
Post-Incident	I	A	R	R	R	C	R	C

Management. Management includes the business managers that are stakeholders in relation to the incident, e.g. the incident involves an information system that their department uses. They are kept informed throughout the process, and provide input into decision making as needed.

CISO and security. The CISO is ultimately accountable for information security incident handling. The members of the information security team are the employees who are trained in the area of handling information security incidents. They are valuable assets not only because of their ability to handle a multitude of incidents, but for their ability to provide options and implications of these options to management and other members of the team. Information security's role includes assessing the scope of the damage, forensics, and recovery.

If faced with an incident that involves direct contact with the system, the security team (which encompasses physical security in many organizations) is the group with the training to assist in this area. Security's role may include the assessment of any physical damage, investigation of physical evidence, and guarding evidence during a forensics investigation to maintain a chain of evidence.

Information technology. Many companies have a separate security and IT department. In the event of an incident, the IT team will need to know where the data can be accessed, and what areas of the network are off-limits. IT's role is to ease the effects to system end users, and to assist the information security team with technical matters as required.

IT Auditor. Many companies are beginning to utilize auditors that are specially trained in the area of computer technology. It is their role within the company to be sure procedures are being followed, and to help drive change when current procedures are no longer appropriate. They will more than likely be present during a crisis, but not take a great deal of action at that time. The IT auditor's role is to observe, learn how the incident came about, ensure procedures are being followed, and work with technical teams to avoid problems in the future. They are important members of the team when conducting post-incident reviews.

Legal. An attorney is useful for providing the CIRT with legal counsel. The attorney's role is to ensure the usability of any evidence collected during an investigation in the event that the company chooses to take legal action. An attorney can also provide counsel regarding liability issues in the event that an incident affects customers, vendors, and/or the general public, etc.

Human resources. Many incidents involve company employees. The Human Resources Department's role is to provide advice regarding how best to handle situations involving employees. HR will generally not be called upon to assist with an incident until after an investigation has begun, and only in the event that an employee is discovered to be involved.

Public Relations. A company's image is an asset of considerable weight and import, especially if the company is publicly traded. When possible, most companies like to keep minor incidents quiet and out of the media, although sometimes this isn't an option. If that information does need to be shared however, the public relations group can best provide advice as to the message that should come from the company, and the best way to communicate that message. The role of the public relations professionals is to communicate with team leaders, ensuring an accurate understanding of the issue and the company's status and, if necessary, to communicate with the press and informing the public and stockholders of the current situation.

In addition to these members, other team members from outside a company might also need to be included. These could include, but are not limited to, professionals such as law enforcement, vendors, and/or technical specialists.

Chapter 4

Review Boards

Internal Controls Review Board

CISOs play a vital role in internal control by ensuring the confidentiality, integrity and availability of systems and information. Internal controls are established to keep the company on course toward profitability goals and achievement of its organizational mission, and to minimize surprises along the way. They promote efficiency, reduce risk of asset loss, and help ensure the reliability of financial statements, and compliance with laws and regulations.[22]

---

[22] COSO. *Internal Control – Integrated Framework Executive Summary*. Retrieved from
http://www.coso.org/documents/Internal%20Control-

The Committee of Sponsoring Organizations of the Treadway Commission (COSO) Board recognizes that management's assessment of internal control is often a time-consuming process that involves a significant amount of management and internal audit testing. Effective monitoring can help streamline the assessment process, but many organizations do not fully understand this important component of internal control. As a result, they underutilize it in supporting their internal control assessments.

Unmonitored controls tend to deteriorate over time. Monitoring, as defined in the COSO framework, is implemented to help ensure "that internal control continues to operate effectively."[23] Over time, effective monitoring

---

Integrated%20Framework.pdf.

[23] COSO. *Guidance on Monitoring Internal Control Systems.* Retrieved from http://www.coso.org/documents/coso_guidance_on_monitoring_intro_online1_002.pdf.

can lead to organizational efficiencies and reduced costs associated with public reporting on internal control because problems are identified and addressed in a proactive, rather than reactive, manner. Organizations may select from a wide variety of monitoring procedures, including but not limited to:

- Periodic evaluation and testing of controls by internal audit

- Continuous monitoring programs built into information systems

- Analysis of, and appropriate follow-up on, operating reports or metrics that might identify anomalies indicative of a control failure

Roles and Responsibilities

Given the scope of the internal controls framework, multiple groups all play a part in related processes.

	Management	CISO	Security	IT	Audit
Development of internal controls framework and policies	A	R	R	R	
Continuous monitoring of system controls	I	A	R	R	
Periodic evaluation and controls testing	I	R	R	R	A
Remediation of findings and tracking to closure	I	A	R	R	R

Management. The CEO is ultimately responsible

and should assume ownership of the system. In a large

company, this role involves providing leadership and

direction to senior managers and reviewing the way the business is controlled. Senior managers, in turn, assign responsibility for establishment of more specific internal control policies and procedures to personnel responsible for the unit's functions. Any findings and deficiencies identified by the Internal Audit department should be addressed and tracked to closure.

Internal Auditors. Internal auditors play an important role in evaluating the effectiveness of control systems, and contribute to ongoing effectiveness going forward.

Other Personnel. Internal control is, to some degree, the responsibility of everyone in the organization and, therefore, should be either an explicit or implicit part of everyone's job description. Practically all employees produce information used in the internal control system or take other actions needed to effect control. Also, all personnel should be responsible for communicating upward problems in operations, noncompliance with the code of conduct, or other policy violations or illegal actions.

A number of external entities often contribute to the achievement of company objectives. External auditors, bringing an independent and objective view, contribute directly through the audit and indirectly by providing information useful to management and the board in carrying out their responsibilities. External parties, however, are not responsible for, nor are they a part of, the company's internal control system.

Change Management Review Board

Corporate networks, information systems, and data centers are in constant flux. While change is a natural and necessary component of network growth, unmanaged change can quickly lead to disorder that exposes critical data and resources to risk. To prevent exposure, change management systems are implemented to help companies ensure that change requirements and approvals are met before a change to the technical environment is implemented. The purpose of change management is to prevent unintended consequences and ensure that changes or alterations to systems are implemented consistently and according to an accepted framework.

As an integrative component in risk management, change extends to include all implications resulting from a particular change. For example, how much downtime will be incurred, what is the cost associated with the change and resulting downtime, will the change impact other systems and/or services, what is the schedule for the change, and will it conflict with any other changes are all questions that need to be addressed and may not be answered by just one person. Due to the complexities of today's network environments, many of the exposures associated with poor change management can be quite complex and subtle. . Networks are complicated environments, and dependencies are not always clear, especially to someone who only sees a small part of the system as a whole. It is, thus, important that all stakeholders be involved in the change management process.

The change management process described as follows identifies the steps required to ensure that all changes are properly requested, evaluated, and approved.

Identify Change. The first step begins with a person or process associated with the information system identifying a need for a change. Multiple individuals, such as owners/administrators or even users, can initiate the change or they may be identified by audit findings or other types of reviews. Once the need for a change has been identified, a change request should be submitted to the appropriate decision-making body, i.e. a change management review board or something similar.

Evaluate Change Request. After initiating a change request, the effects that the change may have on the system or other interrelated systems must be evaluated. The level of risk surrounding the change must also be considered at this point. For instance, the risk may be low due to the low impact and low probability of potential risk events. Other changes may carry higher risk depending on the number of applications, services, and users affected; the risk might also be higher if the change affects a significant part of business-critical systems. Other factors to consider are the duration and scope of the service disruption, the availability of a workaround or contingency options, etc.

Decide on Implementation. Once the change has been evaluated and tested, a decision should be made on whether to approve, deny, or defer the change.

Implement Approved Change Request. Once the decision to implement the change has been made, it should be moved from the test environment into production. If required, the personnel updating the production environment should be separate from those individuals that developed the change in order to provide a greater assurance that unapproved changes do not get implemented into production.

Continuous Monitoring. Change management calls for continuous system monitoring to ensure that it is operating as intended and that implemented changes do not adversely impact either the performance or security posture of the system.

Roles and Responsibilities

Although change management is not traditionally regarded as primarily a security function, security must be involved because of the related security implications and risks. There are many roles associated with implementing an effective change management process, and multiple groups or individuals involved. Note that an individual is not limited to a single role (e.g., an individual can be both the system owner and the change management administrator).

	CIO	System Owner	CISO	Change Management Review Board	IT	Admin
Identification and submission of change		A		I		R
Evaluation of change request	C	I	C	A		R
Decision on implementation	C	I	C	A		R
Implementation of approved change		I			A	R
Continuous monitoring		I			R	

Chief Information Officer (CIO). The CIO is

responsible for setting forth policies concerning change

management, and implementing change management at the

highest level for the organization.

System Owner (Management). The system owner

serves as the authority for all matters of change

management for the system. The system owner is

responsible for developing functional requirements and

verifying that the requirements are implemented appropriately.

CISO. The CISO is primarily responsible for addressing security concerns related to the change management program and for providing expertise and decision support to the Change Management Review Board.

Change Management Review Board. Examples of specific activities that the Change Management Review Board is responsible for are as follows:

- Discussing and resolving change requests that require additional funding or resources to implement
- Ensuring that change requests do not adversely affect any systems or services related to the system or associated systems, subsystems, and facilities

Change Management Administrator. The change

management administrator is responsible for day-to-day

activities, including:

- Documenting and implementing the change

  management plan

- Managing change requests and coordinating

  implementation of changes

- Notifying users of system changes

- Ensuring existence of a process for storing,

  retrieving, and distributing change management

  materials

- Ensuring that an audit trail of changes is

  documented and maintained

Chapter 5

Brand Security

Companies spend years and millions of dollars to build and maintain their reputations. Like many things, brand equity is much harder to build than it is to lose. Hits to brand equity have negative effects on many aspects of a business. As a vector that is getting a lot of traction lately with social media and the movement of many more organizations to the web, CISOs must be prepared to manage the challenge of the lack of trappings on the web that exist with a physical brand that is not on the web. In essence brands can be easily copied and duplicated on the web and it is much easier to spoof a brand on the web than it is to spoof a brand that has not ventured cyberspace, i.e. a physical building.

Phishing and other identity theft incidents can degrade a brand's image both online and offline, exposing the organization further to risk and liability. Identity theft incidents can be phishing (email/website-based attacks), vishing (voice/phone-based scams) or SMShing (SMS/text messaging-based scams). Internet brand and trademark infringements along with other infractions can result in a range of unintended consequences including:

- Misleading consumers and exposing the organization to liability

- Directing consumer traffic from its intended destination, thus reducing potential revenues

- Falsely connecting corporate brands with illegal or offensive activities

- Accidental abuses by authorized resellers or agents can lead to significant financial loses and potentially damage customer relationships

Given the threats associated with phishing, identity theft, brand abuse, intellectual property abuse, social media and mobile applications, it is critical that organizations control online brand representation. Users of the brand within an online setting must be presented with brand validation, which gives the user a level of comfort that it is indeed the brand they intended to visit.

Trust Systems

A certification authority (CA) issues certificates and confirms to other entities that the certificate is valid. People, computers, and applications can all be issued certificates from the CA. Certificate holders use the private key to digitally encrypt data, to digitally sign documents, and to identify themselves, allowing others (i.e., relying parties) to rely upon signatures or assertions made by the private key that corresponds to the public key that is certified. In this model of trust relationships, a CA is a third party that is trusted by both the subject (owner) of the certificate and the party relying upon the certificate.

Each CA has the power to authenticate any website to the end user. If any of these organizations lies or gets compromised, however, users are placed at risk. Two examples of recent attacks demonstrate just how weak this trust model has become[24]:

- In March 2011, an affiliate of the considerably large certificate authority, Comodo, issued fraudulent certificates for domains like mail.google.com,

---

[24] Auerbach, D. (2011). *2011 in Review: Ever-Clearer Vulnerabilities in Certificate Authority System.* Retrieved from https://www.eff.org/deeplinks/2011/12/2011-review-ever-clearer-vulnerabilities-certificate-authority-system.

login.yahoo.com, and addons.mozilla.org. Though the false certificates were detected within days, and the scope of the compromise fortunately was not too extensive, the attack highlighted a major problem of the CA system – some CAs, like Comodo, are too large to fail. If the organization were to be compromised in a serious way, browsers would be faced with the extraordinary task of figuring out which certificates they could trust. Distrusting all of Comodo's certificates would mean that a significant portion of the Internet would be inaccessible to users of the browser, but trusting Comodo too broadly might mean trusting some fraudulent certificates.

- Around July 2011, the CA DigiNotar was compromised, and for several months, hundreds of thousands of users (most of whom appeared to be from Iran) were subject to a man-in-the-middle attack using the fraudulent certificates from DigiNotar. This is the largest known successful attack on the existing CA system to date, and a wake-up call that staying the course is unacceptable for the security of Internet users. A large number of users were affected and their communications on popular sites like Gmail could be read. Browser vendors were able to remove DigiNotar from their respective lists of trusted CAs due to DigiNotar's relatively small size, but the attack went unnoticed for months.

Transitive Trust

Transitive trust is trust transmitted through another party. Transitive trust allows the following: Company A validates and trusts Company B; Company B validates and trusts Company C; Company A trusts but does not need to validate Company C. For example, Company A trusts Company C, but does not perform original entity authentication of Company C.

Consider the following example of transitive trust, which is common in light of the frequency of bank mergers in recent years. Assume being a customer of Bank A, which is acquired by Bank Z. Because Bank Z trusts Bank A's original validation process, there is trust by Bank Z to continue normal banking activities (unless previously allowed activity somehow significantly violates the new owner's security policy). The new portfolio owner has presumably reviewed, very carefully, Bank A's financial statements, security policy, and validation process to have confidence in extending trust to the customers it gains through the acquisition.[25]

Such a trust model is common in distributive or peer-to-peer systems. It relies on participating entities to align their security policies that control credential validation (for example, original entity authentication). Because the company explicitly trusts another entity to perform credential validation, the company should, at the very least, evaluate that entity's security policy, validation process, and position on liability management. The advantage of the transitive trust model is that it enables the linkage of different entities that share similar security policies while reducing the credential validation effort, making the scope

---

[25] Sun Microsystems. (2003). *Trust Modeling for Security Architecture Development.* Retrieved from http://www.informit.com/articles/article.aspx?p=31546&seqNum=3.

of validating users and establishing trust relationships more

manageable.

Chapter 6

Physical Access Security

Much of our critical infrastructure is controlled by cyber-physical systems responsible for monitoring and controlling various processes. The Supervisory Control and Data Acquisition (SCADA) systems for example are industrial control systems responsible for a wide range of industrial processes, such as manufacturing, power generation, and refining. The importance of monitoring and control, which relies heavily on such cyber-physical systems, is paramount to various industrial sectors and ever more increasing smart buildings. Therefore, CISOs play a vital role in ensuring the protection of these systems from attack and compromise.

The year 2010 was a significant period for the security of the industrial software and equipment industry. A computer worm called Stuxnet was targeting highly specialized industrial systems in critical high-security infrastructures. This worm attack demonstrated that, at that time, many of the security assumptions made about the operating environment, technological capabilities, and potential threat evaluations, were far removed from reality. It was considered that a "safe" environment, i.e. disconnected from the Internet and with limited personnel access, was good enough protection. In this case however, removable media acted as a propagation framework. Additionally, although the Programmable Logic Controllers (PLCs) were not connected to the Internet or even the internal network, opportunistic connections (e.g., for reconfiguration, maintenance, or functionality assessment) would be enough to introduce the malicious code. Security clearance on people does not imply security on their accompanying assets. In the Stuxnet case, a trustworthy employee with an unknowingly root-kitted laptop or an infected USB flash drive would have been enough to spread the malware.

Security is a multi-faceted process where solutions focusing asymmetrically on only a few aspects without addressing the rest of the picture may give a false sense of safety and security. Physical access and security, particularly around the data center, is and will always be critical. The data center is a complex environment of physical and virtual systems, and must be integrated and optimized to deliver timely, secure, and trusted information

throughout the organization. Security activities that are
related to this responsibility could include the following:

- *Access and administration*. This function involves
  ensuring that the right users have access to the right
  information in a timely manner, providing
  comprehensive identity management, access
  management, and user compliance auditing
  capabilities.

- *Threat and application security*. This responsibility
  encompasses proactively mitigate and manage data
  center threats including application level
  vulnerabilities, one of today's biggest security
  issues.

- *Data protection*. This includes information security
  assessments to learn where critical data exists,
  where potential security gaps exist, and to develop a

strategy to protect that data. Information protection

services include backing up, restoring, archiving

and maintaining access to critical data with onsite

and remote data protection capabilities for data

center servers, applications and databases, email,

laptops and desktops.

Physical Security and Access Considerations
Some considerations to take into account when

looking at physical security and access, particularly around

data centers, are as follows:

- *Physical location.* Locations are often determined

  by operational and/or technical requirements. A

  backup data center often needs to be located within

  a certain distance of the primary data center. WAN

costs and the capability to replicate between the locations are major factors to ensure that operations remain available. After a location is determined, the following location criteria must be considered:

- Ideally, the building should not be a multi-tenant facility. This reduces the amount of people traffic in and around the building not associated with data center operations.

- The data center building should be outside of a flood zone.

- Downtown areas should be avoided.

- Facilities that are in close proximity to airport flight patterns, railroad tracks, busy thoroughfares, chemical plants, or any other type of facility that is prone to disrupt operations, should be avoided.

- The data center building should be within reasonable commuting distance for employees, support vendors, and other business partners.

- Local ordinances should be reviewed to determine if there might be a potential impact to data center operations (e.g., the use of diesel generators, etc.).

- ***Redundant utility access.*** Data centers need redundant sources of telecommunications (and network circuits), electricity, and water to eliminate any single points of failure.

- ***Power distribution.*** In addition to redundant utilities that support the facility, there needs to be adequate capacity to accommodate growth. Factors that should be considered include maintenance to allow for bypass and emergency shutdowns, and using uninterruptible power supplies (UPS) in conjunction with generators with adequate capacities to run the data center's essential services.

- *Cooling.* HVAC needs to be built to account for future expansion to guarantee that systems do not overheat. The data center heating and cooling systems must be designed to maintain the physical environment of the facility, including cooling, relative humidity, etc. Redundancy of the HVAC system must also be built into the design.

- *Fire detection and suppression.* A comprehensive fire detection and suppression system is a major priority to ensure that both life and property are protected. Local ordinances must be reviewed to determine appropriate options for fire suppression.

- *Video surveillance.* Surveillance cameras should be installed around the perimeter of the building, main entrance, and entry points, as well as at critical entry points within the building. Camera monitoring should be considered when evaluating staffing requirements. Additionally, a method must be established for the storage and retention of videos for forensic purposes.

- *Protection of data center's physical systems.* The data center's physical systems (including generators, cooling systems, etc.) must be in a secure location, and not susceptible to weather events.

- *Layered physical security.* The core of the facility must be kept highly secured. A person should have to go through several levels of authentication before he/she is able to enter the main data center where systems reside.

- ***Development and audit of policies and procedures relating to physical security.*** The physical security policies, programs, and guidelines must be clearly defined. This encompasses the criteria for access, the processes for granting access to employees, visitors, contractors, and certain areas, the process for handling employee transfers and terminations, and emergency and evacuation procedures. Procedures and standards must be tested and audited to ensure they are being followed.

- ***Security awareness of employees.*** Employees should be educated on the policies regarding physical security. This could include activities such as annual training, regular informational emails or

memos, etc.

Chapter 7

Trends in Cyber Security

With the advent of consumerization in business, where technologies are no longer solely owned and managed by corporations, many new trends have surfaced and are slowly becoming the mainstay of operations for organizations. The mostly widely of these trends include rampant use of mobile devices and cloud computing.

Bring Your Own Device (BYOD)

Today's IT and security leaders face many challenges and rapid changes, all while having to do more with less. They must provide end users with the latest, most advanced technologies to remain competitive, all while

protecting the company, customer and employee data and
thwarting attacks from cybercriminals.

New technology brings more channels to access
data, new types of devices, and alternatives to the
traditional PC platform. These dynamics have created a
shift toward BYOD, a trend in the workplace that is rapidly
becoming the rule rather than the exception. BYOD
encompasses more than personal computers. It covers
employees using smart phones, tablets, ultra-light books,
among others to perform daily responsibilities and job
functions. The concept of BYOD broadens to include
software and services, as employees use cloud services and
other tools on the web. Implemented properly, a BYOD
program can reduce costs while increasing productivity and
revenue. As BYOD goes mainstream in IT departments, the

CISO organization should be front and center for users and IT administrators alike.

It is risky to assume that prohibiting personal devices solves the problem, because employees end up using their own devices anyway, unmonitored and undeterred by security policies. Whatever managers think of BYOD and however they choose to implement it, security leaders should treat it the same way as any introduction of new technology – with a controlled and predictable deployment.

All organizations have the flexibility, based on their corporate culture and regulatory requirements, to embrace BYOD as much as they deem reasonable. For example, some companies have decided the risk is too great and have chosen not to implement a BYOD program at all. In May 2012, for instance, IBM banned its employees from using two popular consumer applications over concerns about data security. The company banned cloud storage service Dropbox, as well as Apple's iPhone personal assistant, Siri. Siri listens to spoken requests and sends the queries to Apple's servers where they are deciphered into text, and can also create text messages and emails on voice command – some of which could contain sensitive, proprietary information.[26]

Ultimately, the success of a BYOD program is measured by employees' willingness to use their personal devices within the rules and guidelines set for them. An organization's security procedures and policies should determine whether and how to adopt BYOD, and must be clear and specific on the standards that apply.

---

[26] SOPHOS. *BYOD Risks and Rewards*. Retrieved from http://www.sophos.com/en-us/security-news-trends/security-trends/byod-risks-rewards/what-byod-means-for-business.aspx.

The first and best defense in securing BYODs begins with the same requirements applied to devices that are already on the network. Companies need to have the ability to enforce security policies on a device level and protect their intellectual property if that device is ever lost or stolen. These security measures include:

- Enforcing strong passcodes on all devices

- Antivirus protection

- Full-disk encryption for disk, removable media, and cloud storage

- Mobile device management to wipe sensitive data when devices are lost or stolen

- Application control

Users should be encouraged to think of the extra layers of security as helpful tools that give them the ability to use their own devices within the workplace. It is important to extend encryption to both data in transit and data at rest. Protecting devices with strong passwords means making it more difficult for someone to break in and steal data. But if somehow someone's device-level password is compromised, encrypting the data stored on the device provides a second level of security a hacker must get through in order to steal his/her data.

CISOs should strive for balance and always realize that a successful BYOD program allows users to be productive outside of their scheduled work hours while giving them the flexibility to do the things they often to do when they are not working – such as send messages, update their status on their social networks, or check their personal emails, however, clear policies and training are a leading practice for implementing this strategy.

Mobile Devices

Mobile devices, such as smart phones and tablets, proliferate in today's corporate environments. While there are significant opportunities to leverage these devices to increase the effectiveness of mobile workers, there are also significant concerns about the privacy of sensitive corporate data stored on the devices that IT must handle. The following is a brief picture of the state of mobile device use in companies, and the associated security risks, based on a study conducted by CheckPoint in 2012[27]:

- The use of mobile devices within the corporate setting is rapidly increasing, with 65 percent of

---

[27] Dimensional Research. (2012). *The Impact of Mobile Devices on Information Security.* Retrieved from http://www.checkpoint.com/downloads/products/check-point-mobile-security-survey-report.pdf.

companies allowing personal devices to connect to corporate networks.

- Study participants who say their organizations do allow personal devices to connect to corporate networks cite significant growth in the number of personal devices in the past two years. Of these, the vast majority, 94 percent, say that they have seen an increase in the use of personal mobile devices connecting to corporate networks. The growth has been significant, with 78 percent saying more than twice as many personal devices are used at work compared to two years ago.

- Security risks are on the rise because of mobile devices. Seventy-one percent say mobile devices have contributed to increased security incidents.

- Employee behavior impacts the security of mobile data. Participants were asked what types of corporate information were stored on mobile devices used by employees. The most frequently reported type of information was corporate email (79 percent) and business contacts (65 percent). However, users also reported that a significant level of very sensitive information was on their mobile devices, including customer data (47 percent), network login credentials (38 percent), and corporate information made available through business applications (32 percent).

- Lack of employee awareness about security policies was ranked as having the greatest impact on the security of mobile data, followed closely by

insecure web browsing (61 percent) and insecure
Wi-Fi connectivity (59 percent).

- Participants were asked which group of individuals
  was considered the greatest security risk – careless
  employees or hackers who intentionally try to steal
  corporate information. Significantly more
  participants said careless employees pose a greater
  security risk (72 percent) than hackers (28 percent),
  which reinforces the importance of implementing a
  strong combination of technology and security
  awareness throughout an organization.

Without question, the pervasiveness of BYOD,
mobile apps, and cloud services, has created the gigantic
task of protecting corporate information for businesses both
large and small. An effective mobile security strategy will
focus on protecting corporate information on the multitude

of devices and implementing proper secure access controls for mobile information and applications. Equally important for CISOs is educating employees about best practices, as the majority of businesses are more concerned with careless employees than cybercriminals. Specific examples of security measures that can be taken to reduce associated risks are as follows (similar to recommendations for BYOD):

- Enforce password protection
- Use encryption
- Stay up to date on operating system patches
- Use antivirus software
- Educate users about malicious sites and phone numbers
- Educate users about phishing

Cloud Computing

With cloud computing, there is a significant workload shift and organizations are joining the craze in droves and CISOs should embrace by enabling the business but also weighing the risks and costs and providing the business with the solutions that manage these risks.

Local computers no longer have to do all the heavy lifting when it comes to running applications. Hardware and software demands on the user's side decrease, shifting over to the network of computers on the cloud. The only thing the user's computer needs to be able to run is the cloud computing system's interface software, which can be as simple as a web browser, and the cloud takes care of the rest.

Perhaps the biggest concerns for CISOs about cloud computing are security and privacy. The idea of handing over important data to another company causes worry and concern, with just cause. Corporate executives might hesitate to take advantage of a cloud computing systems because they cannot keep their company's information under lock and key and some business individuals simply decide to do it without any thought of security.

Specific to privacy, if a client can log in from any location to access data and applications; it is possible that the client's privacy could be compromised. Cloud computing companies will need to find ways to protect client privacy. Whether it is a public cloud on the Internet or a private cloud that sits behind a corporate firewall, cloud resources are subject to the same risks as any shared resource, and they require similar protective measures. To leverage the benefits of cloud computing, issues of privacy, authentication, and security must be addressed. A one-size-fits-all approach – one that treats enterprise e-mail the same as uploaded photos, or healthcare data the same as tweets – will not work.

The processing and storage of sensitive and confidential information requires the development and implementation of technical privacy protection measures to implement privacy and security by design. This concept involves building in privacy and security measures from the very outset of a system's development and throughout its life cycle.

Social Media

Social media can offer business advantages for organizations and many are adopting social media as a normal business outlet, yet the concerns for CISOs remain the same. Organizations can use this media to reach out to mass audiences efficiently and at a very low cost.

Organizations can promote brand awareness in many different markets. They can also network with current and potential customers. All this information is a highly valuable asset, and therefore, questions concerning information security become increasingly important.

Cybercriminals continue to use social profile information and the demographics of certain social networking sites to better target their attacks. The proliferation of social networking applications across both the business and home landscapes and the continued blurring of these lines increases the likelihood of weak link attacks on vulnerable sites and content. In many of these cases, attackers are relying on the transitive trust model for a successful attack – with ads, links and widgets appearing on trusted sites that could draw the user to a malicious site and get malware pushed to them.

A dichotomy exists between companies that have embraced the advantages of this new technology and those that mostly avoid it due to associated risks. Social media can have tremendous benefits but also can have serious security risks for organizations. Two of the greatest risks to organizations are malware and inadvertent disclosure of sensitive information. Companies often cite the security risks as a reason they do not allow social media use. Seventy-two percent of companies believe employees' use of social media poses a threat to their organizations.[28]

According to a report by Sophos, the incidence of malware is increasing on the most popular social media sites including Twitter, MySpace, Facebook and LinkedIn. In 2010, 57 percent of users reported they received spam

---

[28] Chi, M. (2011). *Security Policy and Social Media Use.* Retrieved from http://www.sans.org/reading_room/whitepapers/policyissues/reducing-risks-social-media-organization_33749.

via social media sites, an increase of 70.6 percent compared to the previous year. Additionally, 36% percent of users report they were sent malware via social media sites, a rise of 69.8 percent over 2009. Businesses, including small and medium-sized businesses (SMBs), have also been victims of Internet attacks. In a 2009 survey, 24 percent of SMBs reported having been compromised by employees who used social media sites; 25 percent by employees who used peer-to-peer networking sites; and 32 percent by workers who downloaded media. Even companies that strongly believed they devoted sufficient resources to information security reported successful attacks from viruses (60 percent of respondents), spyware (57 percent), and phishing (47 percent). Security breaches against SMBs are particularly troublesome because many of them lack the resources to adequately contain and recover from attacks.

As with all information technologies, organizations must understand the security threats associated with social media and must establish and enforce good policies in order to mitigate the security threats. Protecting online reputations and uncovering opportunities for meaningful consumer conversations require monitoring that focuses on data quality, not quantity – prioritizing what's meaningful, relevant and emotionally charged to mitigate negative impact on an organization or highlight positive feedback. Social media monitoring is a key component of any comprehensive online reputation management effort. This could include: searching websites, blogs, forums, news, and social media sites; identifying information with negative impact, including defamatory comments, sensitive information disclosed, and rumors or inaccuracies; determining the relevance of the sentiments being expressed in social media channels; and prioritizing action based on the sentiments expressed and the authority of the source.

Advanced Persistent Threats (APTs)

Perhaps the biggest challenging threat for CISOs is that of an APT. An APT is a highly organized, purposeful, well-funded attack against a specific target, usually involving a large group of people working together and each bringing their own specialized skills to the table. The word "specific" is very important in this definition because the criminal operators behind an APT have an intended purpose for wanting to target a particular entity. Using different methods, either internal or external, the attacker will relentlessly attempt to gain access to the network and stay there until they have achieved his objective. Though the incidence of these types of attacks is fairly small when compared to automated or commoditized threats that are broad in their targeting, APTs and the actors behind them can pose a much more serious threat.

APTs are typically directed at business and political targets, including government agencies and organizations in industries such as finance, energy, IT, aerospace, and chemical and pharmaceuticals. Users and organizations with access through business relationships to valuable data, such as smaller defense contractors, are also beginning to be targeted.

APTs require a high degree of stealth over a prolonged duration of operation in order to be successful. The attack objectives, therefore, typically go beyond immediate financial gain. Moreover, compromised systems continue to be in service even after key systems have been breached and initial goals reached. Definitions of precisely what an APT is can vary widely, but can best be summarized by their named requirements:

- *Advanced.* Criminal operators behind the threat utilize the full spectrum of computer intrusion technologies and techniques. While individual components of the attack may not be classed as particularly advanced (e.g. malware components generated from commonly available DIY construction kits, or the use of easily procured exploit materials), their operators can typically access and develop more advanced tools as required. Off-the-shelf and commercial malware includes all of the features and functionality necessary to infect digital systems, hide from host-based detection systems, navigate networks, capture and extricate key data, provide video surveillance, along with silent and covert channels for remote control. If needed, APT operators can and will use custom-developed malware tools to achieve specific objectives and harvest information from non-standard systems. They combine multiple attack methodologies and tools in order to reach and compromise their target.

- *Persistent.* Operators give priority to a specific task, rather than opportunistically and immediately seeking immediate financial gain. This distinction implies that the attackers are guided by external entities. The attack is conducted through continuous monitoring and interaction in order to achieve the defined objectives. It does not involve a barrage of regular attacks and malware updates that are immediately detectable.

- ***Threat***. There is a level of coordinated human involvement in the attack, rather than a mindless and automated piece of code. The criminal operators have a specific objective and are skilled, motivated, organized, and well funded.

To achieve their objective, those developing an APT must find vulnerabilities within a target's infrastructure, evaluate the security controls protecting it, determine how to deliver the attack, exploit the vulnerability, compromise the target network, gain access to privileged hosts, find the target data and then extract it – all without being detected. This requires enormous amounts of research, and the entire process may take months or even years.

APTs breach organizations through a wide variety of vectors; despite properly designed and maintained layered security or defense-in-depth strategies. These vectors include:

- **Internet-Based Malware Infections:** drive-by downloads, email attachments, file sharing, pirated software, spear phishing, DNS routing modifications.

- **Physical Malware Infections:** infected USB memory sticks, infected external media such as CDs and DVDs, infected memory cards, infected appliances, backdoored IT equipment

- **External Exploitation:** professional hacking, mass vulnerability exploits, co-location host exploitation, cloud provider penetration, rogue Wi-Fi penetration, smart phone bridging

It is important to note though that well-funded APT adversaries do not necessarily need to breach perimeter security controls from an external perspective. They can, and often do, leverage internal factors such as insider threat and trusted connection vectors to access and compromise targeted systems. Abuse and compromise of trusted connections is a key element for many APTs. While the targeted organization may employ sophisticated technologies and controls in order to prevent the infection and compromise of their systems, criminal operators behind APTs often tunnel in using the hijacked credentials of employees or maybe even business partners or via less-secured remote offices. As such, almost any organization or remote site may fall victim to an APT and be utilized as a soft entry or information harvesting point.

- **Insider Threat:** rogue employee, malicious subcontractor, social engineering expert, funded placement, criminal break-in, dual-use software installation

- **Trusted Connections**: stolen VPN credentials, hijacked roaming hosts, B2B connection tapping, partner system breaches, externally-hosted system breaches[29]

Unlike the majority of malware, which randomly infects any computer vulnerable to a given exploit, APTs target specific organizations with the purpose of stealing specific data or causing specific damage. The Conficker worm, for example, used many advanced techniques but did not target a particular organization. It infected millions of computers in more than 200 countries. In contrast,

[29] First name Damballa. *Advanced Persistent Threats.* Retrieved from https://www.damballa.com/knowledge/advanced-persistent-threats.php.

Stuxnet (as discussed in *Physical Access and Security)* was designed to target a certain type, a certain brand and a certain model of control system.[30] Other examples of APTs include:

- Operation Aurora in 2010, where a zero-day vulnerability in IE 6.0 was used in an attempt to steal intellectual property and gain access to user accounts in Google, Adobe, Symantec, and many other high-profile organizations.

- An attack on RSA in 2011, where the Advanced Persistent Threat (APT) started from a spear phishing email that was sent to a small group of employees at the well-respected security firm. The email contained an Excel file with an attachment

---

[30] Cobb, M. (2013). *Advanced Persistent Threats: The New Reality.* Accessed at http://www.darkreading.com/vulnerability/advanced-persistent-threats-the-new-real/240154502.

that installed a backdoor via an Adobe Flash vulnerability. This backdoor was then used to further infiltrate the system.

Assuming there is a sound and effective information security strategy in place that caters to areas such as IDS/IPS, strong passwords, user awareness and training, an email and social networking usage policy, change management process, end point security solutions, gateway and host-based antivirus protection, and incident response plans, to name but a few, there are specific methods that CISOs can take to reduce the APT risk. These include:

- A Security Information Event Management (SIEM) system for the collection, review and notification of security alerts, as well as the collection and review of audit information pertinent to sensitive data access

- Scanning for security vulnerabilities on a regular basis

- Maintaining a solid patch management process

- Implementing Data Leakage Prevention (DLP) technologies to increase traffic monitoring for malicious outbound activity such as requests to malicious websites, dynamic DNS servers and sensitive file transfer, and scan outbound email and web traffic against a dynamic set of rules to prevent data leaving the organization

- Using behavioral threat analytics to flag subtle yet suspicious outbound traffic that might be indicative of APT activity. Such a system would take a baseline of typical activity and then look for anomalies that are not true to everyday "normal" behavior (e.g. FTP traffic from a department that never uses FTP or network traffic being sent to

servers in a country where the organization has

absolutely no affiliation)

Conclusion

The models expressed in this book are a culmination of thought leadership in information risk management combined with winning process combinations and technological implementations that yield a wider field of view for the aspiring CISO. As with any organization, leadership is about trust and also about being able to inspire the right behaviors, thus information security and risk management are only successful when there is sound leadership at the helm of any organizational information security model. Using these tenets, particularly the leadership model defined in the first chapter, one should fully grasp the importance of influence, change, identification of the value proposition in end-to-end quality of information for the viability of organizations.

As organizations become more visible on the Internet and as people lose more and more of their privacy, there is a growing need for leadership with the right optics and periphery as it relates to information sharing, information gathering and information use. This book provides a set of best practices that enhance the CISOs ability to make sound choices in selecting the right processes to protect the organization and protect its most valuable assets; the people and information related to the people therein.

CISOs should look to expand their reach into organizational processes, especially change management, project management and strategy where decisions are made that impact the entire organization to ensure that tomorrow's future is protected by the embedded CISO today.

INDEX

A

B

D

G

H

I

J

K

L

M

R

S

Tracking or tracing, 81
trademark infringements, 94
transformational leadership, 5
Transitive Trust, 96
transitive trust model, 97, 109
trappings on the web, 94
Trends in Security, 1, 103
Trojan horse programs, 81
Trust Systems, 95
trusted business partner, 10
trusted information, 99
trustworthy employee, 99

U

unacceptable risk, 75
unauthorized data, 60, 61
uncertainty, 6, 47
uncoordinated localization of authority, 37
unintended consequences, 90, 94
US Central Command, 54
US National Institute of Standards and Technology, 20

V

vendors, 17, 23, 31, 62, 86, 96, 100
versatile, 13
Video surveillance, 101
virus infection, 83
Vulnerabilities, 8, 44, 95
vulnerability analysis, 46, 47, 79
Vulnerability Management, 1, 44
vulnerability management program, 45, 47

W

Warm Sites, 75
web of technologies, 17

/zla/ /sb/ 2014

www.ingramcontent.com/pod-product-compliance
Lightning Source LLC
Chambersburg PA
CBHW070924210326
41520CB00021B/6788